BIBLE STUDY COMMENTARY

GALATIANS

Genesis — Leon J. Wood

Exodus — F. B. Huey, Jr.

Leviticus — Louis Goldberg

Numbers — F. B Huey, Jr.

Joshua — Paul P. Enns

Job — D. David Garland

Isaiah — D. David Garland

Jeremiah — F. B. Huey, Jr.

Daniel — Leon J. Wood

Hosea — D. David Garland

Amos — D. David Garland

Malachi — Charles D. Isbell

Matthew — Howard F. Vos

Mark — Howard F. Vos

Luke — Virtus E. Gideon

John — Herschel H. Hobbs

Acts — Curtis Vaughan

Romans — Curtis Vaughan and Bruce Corley

Galatians — Curtis Vaughan

Ephesians — Curtis Vaughan

Philippians — Howard F. Vos

Colossians and Philemon — Curtis Vaughan

The Thessalonian Epistles —John F. Walvoord

The Pastoral Epistles — E. M. Blaiklock

James — Curtis Vaughan

1, 2, 3 John — Curtis Vaughan

GALATIANS

BIBLE STUDY COMMENTARY

CURTIS VAUGHAN

ZONDERVAN
PUBLISHING HOUSE
OF THE ZONDERVAN CORPORATION
GRAND RAPIDS, MICHIGAN 49506

GALATIANS: BIBLE STUDY COMMENTARY
© 1972 by The Zondervan Corporation
Grand Rapids, Michigan

Seventh printing 1981
ISBN 0-310-33543-4

Library of Congress Catalog Number: 72-83874

Printed in the United States of America

To my father-in-law
CHARLES H. WITHERS

Contents

Preface

This brief volume is sent forth with the hope that it may offer guidance to pastors and laymen who desire to gain a better understanding of the message of Galatians. It is designed to be a companion to the epistle and should always be used alongside an open Bible. Technical matters usually discussed in more scholarly works have been deliberately omitted.

I am indebted to the Zondervan Publishing House for requesting the manuscript and am deeply grateful for the patience, courtesy, and kindness with which the editors have treated me in the course of completing the work. Mrs. Frank Brooks, who typed the initial draft, and Mrs. Donald L. Ward, who typed the final draft, both rendered invaluable assistance.

Introduction

Galatians, which fills approximately thirteen or fourteen pages of the Greek New Testament, is really only a small tract. It is not distinguished by literary beauty, its arguments are in places quite elusive, and its thought seems sometimes to be far removed from the issues which confront the modern world. Placed in the context of the great writings of antiquity the letter may to the superficial reader appear to be inconspicuous and unimportant. Few books, however, have more profoundly influenced the minds of men, have so significantly shaped the course of human history, or continue to speak with such relevance to the deepest needs of modern life.

The occasion of Galatians.

The letter was written primarily to counteract the teachings of the Judaizers, who taught that Gentiles, in order to be saved, had first to become Jews. Specifically, these errorists challenged Paul at two points. First, they challenged the truth of his Gospel by asserting that salvation is not of sheer grace, that it comes not by faith alone. They did not deny the need for faith in Christ, but they did teach that faith apart from obedience to the Mosaic law was inadequate for full salvation. Second, they challenged Paul's right to preach the Gospel. That is, they argued that he was not a true apostle and that his teaching carried no authority. This double aspect of the Galatian heresy is never lost sight of in the epistle.

The recipients of Galatians.

This is a question to which the commentaries devote much attention. The problem turns upon the manner in which Paul uses the word "Galatia." In the present Study Guide the matter is discussed briefly in connection with the treatment of the opening paragraph of the epistle.

The date of Galatians.

The date which one assigns to this epistle is determined in large measure by the position which he takes relative to the identity of the first readers. Generally those who subscribe to the North Galatian theory date the epistle in the mid-fifties of the first century. Those who subscribe to the South Galatian theory as a rule date Galatians nearer the time of the Jerusalem Conference (A.D. 49). Among these scholars there is a growing tendency to see Galatians as the first of Paul's extant letters and to date it just prior to the Jerusalem Conference.

The message of Galatians.

Galatians is concerned with the question "What makes a person a Christian?" Is it observance of the Mosaic law? Or is it simple faith in Christ? The answer is pinpointed in Galatians 5:6: "For in Christ Jesus neither circumcision availeth anything, nor uncircumcision; but faith working through love" (ASV). (Romans expounds the same theme more fully.) The epistle is concerned then with the heart of the Gospel, indeed, with the very essence of Christianity. In the apostolic period it sounded the death-knell for the Judaizing controversy and paved the way for the full liberty of the Gospel. Centuries later its message was the dominant theme of the preaching of the Reformers. "The Epistle to the Galatians," said Luther, "is my epistle; I have betrothed myself to it; it is my wife."

Unquestionably the message of Galatians is as urgently needed today as at any time of the past. Our generation, as every other generation, needs to be reminded of the sole sufficiency of Jesus Christ for human redemption. Galatians serves as a clarion call for vital religion rather than formal ritual, for personal submission to a living Savior rather than subscription to a dead creed, for glorying in the cross rather than dependence on self, for a life inspired and controlled by the Spirit rather than one regulated by rules. Several key verses within the book epitomize its major themes. Perhaps the most significant are 1:1; 2:16; 5:1, 6, 13, 14, 25; and 6:14, 15.

**BIBLE STUDY
COMMENTARY**

GALATIANS

CHAPTER 1

The Prologue

(Galatians 1:1-10)

The opening verses of Galatians contain the salutation (verses 1-5) and a statement of the circumstances which occasioned the letter (verses 6-10). To an unusual degree the passage also reflects the apostle's frame of mind at the time of writing and gives a forecast of the contents of the letter. Its three main themes — the divine origin of Paul's apostleship, the sufficiency of Christ's redemptive work, and the new life made possible by the believer's rescue from the present evil age — all are touched upon.

I. THE SALUTATION (1:1-5).

All of Paul's letters begin in much the same way, that is, with a brief description of the writer, an identification of the readers, and a wish for the well-being of the readers. Galatians follows this general pattern, but it is characterized by a certain fullness of statement not found in most of the other letters.

1. *The author* (verses 1, 2a). The writer identifies himself by name ("Paul") and office ("an apostle") and makes mention of his associates at the time of writing ("all the brethren which are with me").

Paul refers to his apostolic office in the salutation of each of his epistles except Philippians, 1 and 2 Thessalonians, and Philemon. Here, however, the matter is given special prominence by the abruptness with which it is introduced and by descriptive phrases which qualify it. The Greek word for "apostle," which means "one sent," was used to denote an authorized ambassador, that is, one commissioned to represent and speak for another. Among the rabbis it was a common saying that "one sent by a man is as the man himself." Paul's use of the word reflects his sense of authority. It was his way of saying to the Galatians that his letter came to them with the full authority of Jesus Christ behind it.

Paul's appointment to apostleship was from God. It came *not from men, neither through man, but through Jesus Christ, and God the Father, who raised him from the dead* (verse 1, ASV). The opening phrases contain two contrasts, one suggested by the prepositions ("from" and "through"), the other brought out by the plural "men" and the singular "man." In addition, there is in the overall statement a contrast betwen "men"/"man" and "Jesus Christ"/"God the Father." The meaning is that the ultimate origin of Paul's apostleship was "not from men" (that is, any group of men such as the Jerusalem apostles), and the means by which it was communicated to him was not "through a man" (that is, any single human being). His commission, like that of the other apostles, came directly "through Jesus Christ, and God the Father." Thus, in reference both to its origin and its instrumentality, the Pauline apostleship was divine, not human. Paul does not here tell us when he received his commission, but the statement of verse 15 suggests that it came in connection with his conversion experience.

In characterizing God as the one "who raised him [Jesus] from the dead" stress is laid on the fact that Paul's call, unlike that of the Twelve, who were commissioned by Christ during His earthly ministry, came from the risen and glorified Christ. The entire description of Paul's apostleship, however, is designed to show that both his and that of the Twelve rest on the same basis. They stand or fall together, for the authority behind the one is the authority behind the other.

Associated with Paul at the time of writing this letter were certain "brethren" (verse 2a) who are not named. There is no way of being absolutely sure of their identity. They obviously had nothing to do with the writing of the letter, for it is written throughout in the first person. The mention of them should be seen as a gesture of courtesy. Associated as they were with the apostle, it is probable that they shared his views and were one with him in affection for the Galatians.

2. *The readers* (verse 2b). This letter, written to a group of Christian assemblies identified simply as "the churches of Galatia," is the only Pauline epistle in which no qualifying epithet is added to the designation of the readers. The Corinthians are "the church of God," "sanctified in Christ Jesus, called to be saints" (1 Cor. 1:2); the Philippians are "saints in Christ Jesus" (1:1); the Colossians are "saints and faithful brethren in Christ" (1:2); the Thessalonians are "the church . . . which is in God the Father and in the Lord Jesus Christ" (1 Thess. 1:1); and so forth. Here there is no title of honor, no mention of graces and privileges. The absence of modifying words and

phrases is an early indication of Paul's distress over the spiritual de-
clension of the Galatians. John Chrysostom, a Christian writer of ancient times, observed this and wrote in his commentary: "Mark how
he [Paul] already shows his deep displeasure here."

All are agreed that the Galatian churches were in that section of
the world that we know as Asia Minor. As to the precise location
within Asia Minor, there are different opinions. The traditional view
is that they were located in the north central part, a section invaded
and settled by the Gauls in the third century B.C. Modern Ankara,
the capital of Turkey, is in this region. Paul is thought to have visited
this part of the world on his second and third missionary journeys
(Acts 16:6; 18:23).

In recent years most scholars have inclined to the view that "Galatia"
is used of the Roman province which bore that name. This included
both ethnic Galatia (described above) and a large area to the south
which included the cities of Antioch (of Pisidia), Lystra, Derbe,
Iconium, and so on. Those who subscribe to this theory feel that the
churches to which this letter was sent were probably those established
by Paul on his first missionary journey (cf. Acts 13-14). The South
Galatian theory was championed by Sir William M. Ramsay and is
held today by most British and American scholars. The North Galatian
theory is still advocated by many continental scholars.

3. *The greeting* (verses 3-5). The greeting contains a prayer (verse
3), a statement (verse 4), and a doxology (verse 5). The prayer is for
"grace" and "peace" to be experienced by the readers. Luther spoke
of grace as that which "releaseth sin" and peace as that which "maketh
the conscience quiet." The Greek word for "grace" means essentially
"that which causes joy," but the word came to mean any free gift.
In the New Testament it usually denotes the divine favor.

Williams thinks that "peace" is used to refer "chiefly to external
peace, God's protection encircling believers" (p. 14). Among the
Jews the word had a connotation of wholeness or well-being. Morris
therefore defines it as "prosperity in the widest sense, especially prosperity in spiritual things" (*Thessalonians*, p. 33).

Verse 4, an expansion of the greeting, makes a statement concerning the redemptive work of Christ. He *gave himself for our sins, that
he might deliver us from this present evil world, according to the will
of God and our Father.* At least three matters are emphasized: First,
Christ's atoning work consisted in the giving of Himself, that is, in
the laying down of His life in death for our sins. The words "gave
himself" put stress upon the voluntary nature of Christ's death. "For

our sins" means that Christ's death was a sacrifice made necessary by our sins and offered with a view to their removal. In the Greek version of the Old Testament a similar expression was used for sin-offerings. The closest parallel to this statement in Paul is 1 Corinthians 15:3, "Christ died for our sins."

Second, the purpose of Christ's sacrifice was to "deliver us out of this present evil world" (verse 4b, ASV). The verb "deliver," says Lightfoot, "strikes the keynote of the epistle" (p. 73). Used by Paul only in this place, it means "to pluck out" (cf. Matt. 5:29), "to rescue from danger" (cf. Acts 12:11; 23:27), or "to deliver from bondage" (cf. Acts 7:10, 34; 26:17). The present passage seems to combine the ideas of rescue from danger and deliverance from bondage.

That from which believers are delivered is "this present evil world." "World" is more literally "age," that is, the world considered in reference to time rather than in reference to space. The Jews customarily distinguished between "this age," a period dark and evil, and "the age to come," the glorious Messianic era. The New Testament reflects this same concept, setting the "present age" (cf. Rom. 12:2; Eph. 2:2; 1 Tim. 6:17) over against "the age to come" (Matt. 12:32, Mark 10:30, et al.). The former is under the domination of Satan, the god of this world (2 Cor. 4:4); the latter, which already has been introduced and whose benefits Christians already experience in foretaste (Heb. 6:5), is under the control of Jesus Christ.

The position of the Greek word for "evil" makes it somewhat emphatic. Lightfoot renders it "[the world] with all its evils" (p. 73). Bruce understands the whole construction to mean "the present course of the world, dominated as it is by evil."

Third, Christ's redemptive work was in accordance with "the will of God" (verse 4c). The thought is that both the self-sacrifice of Christ and the purpose in that sacrifice flowed from the divine will. That is to say, it was God's will that we be delivered, and it was His will that this be accomplished by the redemptive deed of Christ. Christ, therefore, did not die in order to gain God's love for us but because God already loved us and willed to save us.

Verse 5 is a doxology, doubtless called forth by the mention of the mercy of God in the preceding verse. Some commentaries call attention to the fact that it was a custom of the rabbis to add a doxology whenever the name of God was mentioned. With Paul, however, the use of the doxology was an expression of real feeling, not mere obedience to a custom (cf. Rom. 11:36; 16:27; Eph. 3:20, 21, etc.).

The verse may be taken either as a prayer (a wish) or as an affirmation. If it is a prayer, it is a request that "glory" (in the sense of praise, honor) may be ascribed to God "for ever and ever" by His creatures. If the verse is an affirmation it asserts that "glory" (in the sense of splendor, radiance) is an essential attribute of God for ever.

II. THE OCCASION OF THE LETTER (1:6-10).

The salutation in Paul's letters is followed ordinarily by an expression of gratitude and appreciation for the readers. Even when writing 1 Corinthians, in which there are many harsh things said of the Corinthian church, Paul begins with a grateful acknowledgement of their wealth of spiritual gifts. In Galatians, however, the apostle begins with an indignant remonstrance and pronounces an anathema (a curse) upon anyone who dares to preach a gospel other than that preached by him.

The paragraph is developed in such a way that it gives us insight into the conditions which created the occasion for writing this letter. Mention is made of (1) the defection of the Galatians (verses 6, 7a), (2) the arrival in Galatia of "some" who were perverting the Gospel of Christ (verses 7b-9), and (3) a malicious assault (doubtless by the same teachers of error) on Paul's personal integrity (verse 10).

1. *The defection of the Galatians* (verses 6, 7a). Paul is alarmed about the situation in Galatia, and he expresses himself with startling vehemence: *I marvel that ye are so soon removed from him that called you into the grace of Christ unto another gospel* (verse 6). "I marvel," which denotes surprise at the unexpected, translates a word used by Paul only here and in 2 Thessalonians 1:10. In the latter passage it expresses pleasurable surprise; here, combining the ideas of astonishment and bewilderment, it denotes painful surprise. Norley translates it, "I am dumbfounded."

"So soon" may refer to the short time which had transpired since the conversion of the Galatians. On the other hand, the suggestion may be that the Galatians' defection had come soon after the arrival of the false teachers. In that case Paul is expressing surprise at the ease with which the Galatians have shifted their loyalty. Weymouth translates it "so readily."

"Are . . . removed," which represents a Greek present tense verb, would be better rendered by an English continuous present, such as "are . . . turning away from" (Goodspeed), "are moving away from" (Rotherham), "are . . . deserting" (Weymouth). The present tense shows that the defection of the Galatians was not yet final and complete; it was a process still going on. Paul's hope in writing this letter was to arreest the process and avert spiritual disaster. The verb itself was used in secular literature of military desertions, of political revolts, of changes in religious opinion, of defections in morals, and so on. In 2 Maccabees 7:24 it is used of turning away from the customs of one's ancestors. Liddell and Scott cite the case of Dionysius of Heraclea, who went over from the Stoics to the Cyrenaics and was called a "turncoat" (translating another form of the Greek word used here). The Galatians, then, were in process of becoming "turncoats."

Their defection was from God ("him that called you") to "another gospel." The Greek word rendered "another" denotes a qualitative distinction, "another of a different kind." Some versions attempt to bring this out in translation. The ASV, for instance, has "a different gospel" instead of KJV's "another gospel." Verse 7a shows that it was "different" because it was really no gospel at all (cf. TCNT). "Gospel" means "good news," but what the Galatians were being asked to accept was a message of bondage. Such a message was a perversion ("a travesty," Phillips) of the good news. The TEV expresses it clearly: "Actually, there is no 'other gospel,' but I say it because there are some people who are upsetting you and trying to change the gospel of Christ."

2. *The heresy of the Judaizers* (verses 7b-9). Paul has expressed his amazement at the instability of the Galatians (verses 6, 7a). Now he denounces those who are leading them astray. Their identity is not made known, but Paul does describe their activity (verse 7) and pronounce their doom (verses 8, 9).

In reference to their activity two things are said: first, they "trouble" the Galatians. The Greek word, which was used in secular writings of physical agitation, mental disturbance (e.g., fear, excitement, confusion), and military and political activity (e.g., throwing into disorder, inciting revolt, etc.), is found more than fifteen times in the New Testament (e.g., Matt. 2:3; John 5:7; 14:1; Gal. 5:10). Burton understands it here in the sense of mental disturbance. Guthrie thinks the context, which employs the metaphor of desertion, lends support to the idea of seditious activity. The NAB says, "Some . . . must have confused you."

Second, they *pervert the gospel of Christ* (vs. 7b). The Greek word suggests a change from one thing to another; more specifically it means "to reverse," that is, *"change to its very opposite"* (Plummer, p. 428). In Acts 2:20 it is used of the sun being "turned into darkness"; in James 4:9, of laughter being "turned to mourning" and of joy being turned to heaviness. In light of what we are told elsewhere in the epistle we may conclude that the persons Paul had in mind were "Judaizers." These were Jews who professed to be Christians but taught that Gentiles in order to be saved had first to submit to the ritual of the Mosaic law. Thus, they perverted the Gospel by substituting a doctrine of salvation by works for a doctrine of salvation by grace. (The controversy created by the Judaizing heresy is dealt with in Acts 15.)

Having described the pernicious activity of the Judaizers, Paul now pronounces a curse upon them — and upon anyone else who would distort the Gospel. *But though we, or an angel from heaven, should preach unto you any gospel other than that which we preached unto you, let him be anathema* (vs. 8, ASV). This should not be interpreted as an outburst of personal anger. As Guthrie states, "It was not an issue of personal prestige. The essence of the gospel itself was at stake" (p. 64). The reasoning is that there is only one authentic Gospel, and it is Christ's (see verse 7). Because it is Christ's it is complete, final, and unchangeable.

"But though" means "even if" or "even though," suggesting a very remote contingency. "We" refers to Paul and those associated with him in the original mission to Galatia. "Or an angel from heaven" shows the unbounded confidence of Paul in the truth of his message. Even a messenger claiming the highest conceivable authority must be rejected if what he says is subversive to the Gospel preached originally to the Galatians by the apostle. "Any gospel other than that which we preached" may mean either of two things: (1) any gospel *besides* or *in addition to* that which we have preached, or (2) any gospel *contrary* to that which we have preached (cf. NEB: "at variance with"). Most recent interpreters decide for the latter meaning.

"Accursed (KJV) is the rendering of the Greek word *anathema* (cf. ASV). Originally, it was used of anything devoted to God — whether in a good sense, that is, for God's service (as the sacrifices, Lev. 27:28), or in a bad sense, that is, for destruction (as the city of Jericho, Josh. 6:17). Later, the word took on the more general sense of the disfavor of God, and it is in this sense that it is used here. Thus the sentence expresses Paul's feeling that anyone who perverts the Gospel should for so doing incur the wrath of God. The NEB has, "he shall be held outcast." The TEV renders it, "may he be condemned to hell!" Phillips puts it, "may he be damned!" The extreme language reveals the seriousness with which Paul viewed the differences between Christ's Gospel (preached by the apostle) and the message of the Judaizers.

Verse 9 repeats the thought of the preceding verse, the repetition

serving to stress the gravity of the matter under discussion. The
wording, however, is slightly altered. Verse 8, for instance, is in the
form of a future supposition. That is, it envisions a hypothetical situation. The grammar of verse 9 is changed so as to describe a present,
concrete situation.

As we said before (verse 9) presumably does not refer to the statement of the preceding verse but to oral pronouncements made by
Paul on an earlier visit. That the apostle had thus warned the Galatians suggests that there were even then some apprehensions of
trouble. Moreover, the fact that the Galatians had been forewarned
made their reception of the false teachers more culpable. They knew
that a false gospel involved an anathema, but in spite of this knowledge they were following those who preached such a gospel. *Any man*
is literally "any one"; thus the statement is general enough to include
angels as well as men.

3. *The attack on Paul's personal integrity* (verse 10). Verse 10 implies that Paul's opponents had accused him of courting the favor of
men, of being a compromiser. They may have seized upon Paul's having Timothy circumcised as a basis for charging that he was not above
accommodating himself to Jewish prejudice or heathen customs as the
occasion demanded. (The same allegation is dealt with in 5:11.) Paul
was indeed willing to make many concessions to those he sought to
win, so long as no vital issue was at stake (cf. 1 Cor. 9:19-23; Acts
21:17-26). But where the truth of the Gospel was the issue, he would
entertain no thought of compromise. The present passage testifies to
that. In effect, Paul says: "Read what I have just written. Does that
sound like the utterance of one who is trying to ingratiate himself
with men? My only concern is to please God."

The first part of verse 10 contains two rhetorical questions: *For do
I now persuade men, or God? or do I seek to please men?* The TEV
expresses the drift of the first question: "Does this sound as if I am
trying to win men's approval? No! I want God's approval!" The second
question, added for the sake of emphasis, employs a verb which suggests currying favor with a view to being popular. TEV: "Am I trying
to be popular with men?" Paul does not answer either question, but
the reply is obvious. It is God's approval that he seeks, and he does
not court the favor of men. The last half of verse 10 enforces this
thought by affirming that the desire to please men (i.e., curry favor
with them) and the desire to serve Christ are incompatible. *If, after
all these years, I were still courting the favour of men, I should not
be what I am, the slave of Christ"* (Knox's translation). The apostle's

pre-conversion life might have been characterized by a desire to win the approval of men, but as a Christian his consuming passion was to serve Christ. Paul's words are a sort of reiteration of the words of our Lord that "No man can serve two masters" (Matt. 6:24).

For Further Study

1. Read Galatians in a translation you have not used before. Watch for distinctive words and phrases.

2. Read the accounts of Paul's three missionary journeys in the Book of Acts.

3. Read articles on "Galatia," "Apostle," and "Gospel" in *The Zondervan Pictorial Bible Dictionary* (or some other similar work).

4. In Charles H. Spurgeon's *Treasury of the New Testament* (published by Zondervan) there are eleven sermons on texts in Galatians.

CHAPTER 2

The Apostleship of Paul:

Independent of the Jerusalem Apostles

(Galatians 1:11-24)

The main body of the Epistle to the Galatians, which begins with 1:11, may be divided into three sections of almost equal length. The first (1:11 – 2:21) is autobiographical, setting forth a defense of Paul's apostolic authority. The second (chapters 3 and 4) is polemical, giving an exposition of the truth of his Gospel. The third (5:1 – 6:10), the especially practical portion of the book, unfolds the nature of the Christian life.

These three themes already have been briefly touched upon – the first in 1:1, the second in 1:4 (cf. 1:8, 9), the last in 1:4b. Indeed, to a remarkable degree the first two seem to be present in almost every paragraph of the letter. Paul was convinced that his Gospel and his apostleship would stand or fall together. He knew in fact that the assault on his authority was an attempt to discredit and destroy the Gospel which he preached.

The first major section of the letter (1:11 – 2:21), which is a carefully stated defense of Paul's apostleship, is intensely personal. Findlay, who calls Galatians 1 and 2 Paul's *apologia pro vita sua,* affirms that they (along with portions of 2 Corinthians, and scattered passages in other letters) form an autobiography of the apostle. "They furnish," he says, "an indispensable supplement to the external and cursory delineations given in the Acts of the Apostles" (p. 54).

Throughout this portion of his letter Paul is answering the charge that his apostleship is not authentic because the Jerusalem apostles had never authorized him as a teacher of the Christian Gospel. He counters this accusation with a threefold argument: first, he avows that his apostleship is not dependent on human authorization, that it is derived, like that of the Twelve, directly from Christ (1:11-24). Second, he points out that the validity of his commission was acknowledged by the Jerusalem apostles and he himself was recognized by

24

them as an equal (2:1-10). Third, he explains how on one notable occasion his authority had been asserted against Peter, who was the reputed leader of the Twelve (2:11-21).

In the section now under consideration (1:11-24) Paul affirms his complete independence of all human authority and contends that he is a divinely-taught, divinely-commissioned apostle. To prove his point he mentions (1) the origin of his Gospel (verses 11, 12), (2) the circumstances of his conversion and call (verses 13-16a), and (3) the events following his conversion (verses 16b-24).

I. THE DIVINE ORIGIN OF PAUL'S GOSPEL (1:11, 12).

Paul begins by affirming the divine origin of his Gospel. *For I make known to you, brethren, as touching the gospel which was preached by me, that it is not after man. For neither did I receive it from man, nor was I taught it, but it came to me through revelation of Jesus Christ* (verses 11, 12, ASV). The statement is given a somewhat formal and solemn character by the introductory verb ("I make known"; cf. 1 Cor. 12:3; 15:1; 2 Cor. 8:1). It draws special attention to the subject about to be presented and indicates that Paul looks upon it as having particular importance. Compare NEB: "I must make it clear to you." Ridderbos says the expression suggests "something remarkable and impressive" (p. 56).

Four assertions, of which three are negative and one is positive, are made: first, Paul asserts that his Gospel (i.e., the good news as preached by him) "is not after man" (verse 11b). Literally, the Greek says "not according to man." That is to say, man is not its measure, its standard, or its pattern. The RSV reads: "the gospel which was preached by me *is not man's gospel.*" That is to say, it is not a human, but a superhuman system. It is not a product of man's inventiveness and genius; it is a creation of the mind of God.

Second, Paul did not "receive it from man" (verse 12a). This assertion is proof of the non-human character of Paul's Gospel. The pronoun preceding the word "receive" is emphatic — "I, though not one of the Twelve." The Greek verb, which is the usual one for receiving a tradition handed down by others, was used in Jewish circles of transmitting oral traditions through the rabbinical schools. Paul's use of it here is intended to affirm that his knowledge of the Gospel did not come through ordinary channels of human tradition. Man was not the source from which he received it, nor was man the means by which it was communicated to him.

Third, Paul was not "taught" the Gospel (verse 12b). This means that human instruction was not the method by which he obtained his Gospel. The statement is very similar to the one immediately preceding. Guthrie observes, however, that "a subtle difference of meaning is implied. Paul wishes to exclude the idea of any private human interpretation" (p. 67).

Fourth, it came to him "by revelation of Jesus Christ." That is to say, it was by a direct revelation similar to that by which God spoke to the prophets of old that Paul came to know the Gospel. This does not necessarily mean that all the facts of our Lord's life and ministry were communicated to Paul in this manner. It does mean that his Gospel, which is an interpretation of those facts, came by divine revelation. The word "revelation" signifies "an uncovering," "an unveiling," "a disclosing." In the New Testament it is used always of a disclosure of religious truth previously unknown.

The precise meaning of the phrase "of Jesus Christ" is not certain, there being two possible ways of interpreting it. That is to say, the words may represent Christ as the One revealed, or they may mean that Christ was the agent through whom the revelation came. Both interpretations yield a good sense, but the former is to be preferred. The thought is that Jesus Christ had been revealed to Paul in such a way that the revelation carried with it the substance of the Gospel. Guthrie, who subscribes to this interpretation, says Paul was "thinking of the whole content of what had been revealed to him as being summed up in Christ" (p. 67). Hunter writes that "Jesus Christ was revealed to him in such a way that he now had a gospel to preach" (pp. 15, 16).

When did this revelation occur? One's answer to this question will to a large extent be determined by his understanding of the words discussed immediately above. Those who take Jesus Christ to be the subject (content) of the revelation see here a reference to the Damascus road experience. On the other hand, those who interpret "of Jesus Christ" to mean that Christ was the agent in the revelation, tend to give a broader, more inclusive answer. Paul's assertion, they say, includes the partial revelation of Christian truth communicated to him when Jesus appeared to him on the road to Damascus, but it should not be confined to this. They argue that the tone of the following verses, especially verse 17, suggests that the revealing work in which the Gospel was made known to Paul included the period spent in Arabia. There is much to be said for this, but on the whole it seems better to confine the revelation to the Damascus road experience.

II. The circumstances of Paul's conversion and call (1:13-16).

Having affirmed the divine origin of his Gospel as one proof of the independence of his apostleship, Paul now narrates the circumstances of his conversion and call as further proof. He mentions first the direction of his life prior to conversion (verses 13, 14) and then describes the nature of his experience which made him a Christian (verses 15, 16a).

1. *Paul's pre-conversion life* (verses 13, 14). In these verses the apostle shows that previous to his conversion he was not at all under Christian influence and was in no way inclined to the acceptance of Christianity. *For ye have heard of my conversation in time past in the Jews' religion, how that beyond measure I persecuted the church of God, and wasted it: And profited in the Jews' religion above many my equals in mine own nation, being more exceedingly zealous of the traditions of my fathers* (verses 13, 14). The matters emphasized are Paul's determined opposition to the Church (verse 13), his progress in the religion of the Jews (verse 14a), and his zeal for the traditions of his fathers (verse 14b). All of this is submitted as evidence (note "for," verse 13) that he had no direct Christian influence upon him before his conversion. Those who might have been his teachers in the Gospel at that time were in fact his opponents and the objects of his persecuting zeal. This zeal, he makes clear, was an expression of his intense devotion to the ancestral traditions of his people.

Paul assumed that this aspect of his life was common knowledge among the Galatians ("ye have heard," verse 13), but we are not told how they had come to have this information. Probably Paul had talked of it during his visits with them.

"Conversation" means manner of life, conduct. Here it refers to Paul's whole way of life. Weymouth: "my early career." "The Jews' religion" translates a single Greek word which occurs in Paul's epistles only here and in the next verse. The rsv has "Judaism," which is a transliteration of the Greek word. The word "church," which most frequently in the New Testament is used of a local congregation of believers, here has reference to the Christian community at large. In saying he "wasted" the church, Paul uses a word which means "to devastate," "to destroy," "to ruin." The asv renders it "made havoc"; Coneybeare, "strove to root it out." The tense of the verb emphasizes the continuing and intensive character of the action — he was "continually trying to destroy" the church.

Verse 14 suggests that before his conversion Paul was perhaps the most promising young Pharisee of his day. The word for "profited" (verse 14a), which literally suggests cutting one's way in a forward direction (cf. "blazing a trail"), is more accurately rendered "was advancing." The NEB uses the word "outstripping." "My equals in mine own nation" were Paul's "Jewish contemporaries" (NEB), probably his fellow students of Jewish law and customs.

2. *Paul's conversion experience* (verses 15, 16a). The apostle's conversion is next described, and the language is carefully chosen to emphasize divine initiative in it all. *It pleased God, who separated me from my mother's womb, and called me by his grace, to reveal his Son in me, that I might preach him among the heathen* (verses 15, 16a).

Everything is traced back to the action of God; He it was who set Paul apart, called him through His grace, and was pleased to reveal His Son in him. The point is that one who had been dealt with in this fashion could in no wise be dependent on men for his knowledge of the Gospel nor his commission to preach it. Nearly every word is significant, but only the key expressions can be treated.

"It pleased God," which translates a single Greek word, grounds the whole experience in the predestinating purpose of God. The noun form ("good pleasure") came almost to be a technical term for the good-will of God to man. The word in our text conveys the thought of a kindly or gracious purpose. Hunter acknowledges that the doctrine of election has at times been so perverted as to bring it into disrepute, but he argues that "the doctrine is not absurd and untenable as its mockers suppose. Is it not," he asks, "basically the belief that we do not just *happen* to exist, that our life has its roots in eternity, and that our salvation begins in the mind of the eternal God . . .? What election means in simple terms is this: God chooses us before we choose Him; God does not choose us because we deserve it; and God does not choose us to be His favorites but to be His servants" (pp. 16, 17).

"Separated me" has reference to God's devoting Paul to a special work, that is, the preaching of the Gospel to Gentiles (cf. Acts 13:2; Rom. 1:1). The Greek word, which means "to mark off from something else" or "to separate or set apart from others," was used especially of setting apart for a particular service.

"From my mother's womb" is understood by some (Burton, Phillips, et al.) in the sense of "from birth." Others (TCNT, RSV) take it to mean "before I was born."

"Called" may refer to the call to apostleship or it may be understood as referring to the call to be a Christian (Rom. 8:30). Williams feels that the term includes "the whole summons of which the revelation (to be mentioned immediately) was the culminating point" (p. 25).

The essence of Paul's experience is expressed in the words, "to reveal his Son in me" (verse 16a). It is much debated whether they refer to a revelation made *to* him or to a revelation made *through* him to others. The first view seems to fit the context better. Burton, who argues for it, points out that "the whole subject of discourse in this paragraph is not how Paul make known his gospel, but how he received it" (p. 51). The representation of the revelation as a revelation "in" Paul in no way rules out the kind of objective and external manifestation described in Acts 9, 22, and 26. Here Paul is simply emphasizing that aspect of it which is pertinent for his argument, namely, that he was inwardly enlightened concerning Christ. Some interpreters suggest that there was an external revelation on the road to Damascus and an inward revelation in the period of seclusion which followed that experience. They feel that Paul's language in the present passage is general enough to take in the whole experience.

The revelation was not an end in itself. Its final purpose was that Paul "might preach [Christ] among the heathen [Gentiles]." The verb employed means "to announce good news," and the substance of this good news is Jesus, God's Son. "Among the Gentiles" (asv) defines the divinely intended sphere of Paul's preaching. He does not make clear whether or not this conception of his work came at the time of his conversion or at some later period. However, the impression conveyed by the narrative is that it came in connection with the conversion (cf. Acts 9:15; 22:15; 26:16-18).

III. The events following Paul's conversion (1:16b-24).

Paul has shown that the facts relating to the source of his Gospel and the circumstances of his conversion and call are all evidences of the independence of his apostleship. Now the events which followed that conversion are narrated to give further evidence. These events are (1) the visit to Arabia (verses 16b, 17), (2) the first visit to Jerusalem (verses 18-20), and (3) the ministry in Syria and Cilicia (verses 21-24).

1. *The visit to Arabia* (verses 16b, 17). Paul stresses that the first thing he did after his life-changing experience was to go away into Arabia: *Immediately I conferred not with flesh and blood: Neither went I up to Jerusalem . . . ; but I went into Arabia*" (verses 16b, 17). "Immediately" should probably be understood as modifying not sim-

ply the first statement (verse 16b), but also the two statements which
follow (verse 17). Paul first asserts what he did not do and then
what he did do in the period immediately following his conversion.
Lightfoot expresses the sense correctly: "Forthwith instead of confer-
ring with flesh and blood . . . I departed," etc. The point of the entire statement is that the apostle "acted from the outset under the
sense of a unique Divine call, that allowed of no human validation or
supplement" (Findlay, p. 77). The word "immediately" is not, of
course, to be so insisted upon as to make it contradict the statement
in Acts that Paul abode three days in Damascus and was ministered
to by Ananias.

"Flesh" was a common Hebraism for "man." Probably the fuller
expression, "flesh and blood," means the same thing. The thought,
then, is that Paul did not turn to any human being for counsel. Compare Matthew 16:17, "Flesh and blood hath not revealed it unto thee."

"Them which were apostles before me" (verse 17) were the Jerusalem apostles, that is, the Twelve (and possibly also James the Lord's
brother). Paul's manner of referring to them not only indicates his
recognition of their apostleship; it also implies that he looked upon
his apostleship as being essentially the same in character as theirs.

"Arabia" was the term applied to the vast peninsula that lies between the Red Sea on the southwest and the Persian Gulf and the
Euphrates River on the northeast, extending to the ocean on the
southeast. Burton points out that "its northwestern boundary was
somewhat vague, but the term generally included the Sinaitic peninsula and excluded Palestine and Phoenicia" (p. 57). We have no way
of knowing precisely which part of Arabia Paul visited. Lightfoot and
others argue for the region about Sinai, which was east and south of
Palestine. The view most commonly held is that Paul went into
some section of Arabia not far from Damascus, perhaps the Nabatean
kingdom, over which Aretas IV was ruler (cf. 2 Cor. 11:32). Burton
feels that "there is nothing to necessitate the supposition that he went
far from Damascus, nor anything to exclude a far-distant journey except that if he had gone far south, a return to Damascus would perhaps have been improbable" (p. 58).

No specific statement is given as to the purpose of Paul's journey
into Arabia. Some have contended that his intention was to preach
the Gospel to the people of that area, but a better view is that he went
away for the purpose of communing with God and reflecting on the
radically different direction into which his life had been turned. This
journey to Arabia is not mentioned by Luke in Acts, but it is not

impossible to fit it into his narrative — perhaps between verses 22 and 23 of chapter 9. Findlay observes that Luke's silence about the sojourn in Arabia was intentional. "The Arabian retreat," he explains, "formed no part of the Apostle's public life, and had no place in the narrative of the Acts" (p. 80).

Again, there is nothing specifically stated as to the length of Paul's stay in Arabia. Verse 18 makes clear that it could not have been more than three years; Hovey thinks that it was probably not less than two years (cf. Acts 9:20-23).

From Arabia Paul *returned again unto Damascus* (verse 17). This is his first mention of Damascus, and the reference to returning "again" would seem strange were we not familiar with the record in Acts. Ridderbos explains that "Paul writes about this period of his life as he would about a matter whose background (the event on the way to Damascus) his readers already knew about in broad outline" (p. 66). At any rate, the word "again" connects his conversion experience with Damascus and implies that it was from Damascus that he had gone away into Arabia. It might have been expected that he would go back to Jerusalem, but he did not. Doubtless this fact is stated in order to stress once more Paul's lack of contact with the Jerusalem Christians in these early, formative years of his Christian life.

2. *The first visit to Jerusalem* (verses 18-20). The next event in Paul's narrative is his return to Jerusalem. *Then after three years I went up to Jerusalem to see Peter, and abode with him fifteen days. But other of the apostles saw I none, save James the Lord's brother* (verses 18, 19). The reference is probably to the visit mentioned in Acts 9:26, which took place after the apostle had narrowly escaped death at the hands of unbelieving Jews in Damascus. Paul calls attention to several features of this visit which underscore his contention that men had nothing to do with his Gospel nor with his commission to preach it. "He was," as Burton says, "conscious of a source of truth independent of men" (p. 58).

For one thing, the visit occurred "after three years" — that is, three years after his conversion. The fact that this much time elapsed between that experience and the first contact that he had with the Jerusalem apostles shows his complete independence of them.

Next, the purpose of this trip was "to visit Cephas" (verse 18, ASV). "Visit" translates a word which means "become acquainted with." Paul went to Jerusalem, then, simply to get acquainted with Peter, not to be instructed by him nor to receive authorization from him. Verse 19 explains that James the Lord's brother was the only other apostle seen on this occasion. James did not, of course, belong to the Twelve, but he is nonetheless reckoned as an apostle (cf. 1 Cor. 15:5). He is mentioned in Matthew 13:35 and Mark 6:3 as one of the brothers of Jesus. It appears that he did not believe in Jesus as the Messiah until after the resurrection of Jesus (1 Cor. 15:7; Acts 1:14). Following his conversion he soon became a leader among the Jerusalem Christians and was thought of as one of the pillars of the church in that city (Gal. 2:9). He is likely the person who wrote the Epistle of James, and it was he who presided over the Jerusalem conference recorded in Acts 15.

Finally, Paul mentions the shortness of the time which he spent in the city. He was there with Peter for only "fifteen days" (verse 18). Acts 9:28 shows that during the entire fifteen day period Paul was "going in and going out at Jerusalem" and was preaching "boldly in the name of the Lord." Thus, the fifteen day period, though affording opportunity for some conversation with Peter about Christ, was surely too short for any thorough study of Christian truth under the instruction of Peter. "The Galatians could not possibly believe that such knowledge as he possessed of the way of life through Christ had been gained in a fortnight from any human teacher" (Hovey, p. 22).

Verse 20, which is introduced parenthetically, is a solemn assertion of the truth of what Paul has just written. *Now the things which I write unto you, behold, before God, I lie not.* Moffatt: "I am writing to you the sheer truth, I swear it before God!" Similar affirmations are found in 1 Thessalonians 2:5; 2 Corinthians 1:23 and 11:31. The fact that Paul thus appeals to God as his witness is an indication of the depth of his feelings about the matter under discussion. The integrity of his whole life's work was at stake. The use of such strong language may also imply that Paul had been charged with misstating the facts about his contacts with the other apostles.

3. *The ministry in Syria and Cilicia* (verses 21-24). The purpose of these verses is to show that for a period of at least eleven years, and possibly for as long as fourteen years (cf. 1:18 and 2:1), Paul was completely out of touch with the other apostles, carrying on his work as a preacher in a section quite remote from Jerusalem. *Afterwards [i.e., after the aforementioned visit to Jerusalem] I came into the regions of Syria and Cilicia* (verse 21). Syria was the province in which Damascus was located and of which Antioch was the capital. In reality Palestine was a part of the province (cf. Luke 2:2), but the context seems to require us to interpret "Syria" here in a narrower fashion. Paul may have been thinking particularly of Antioch and its

environs. We know from Acts (11:25ff) that he was engaged in ministry there. "Cilicia" was the province in which Tarsus, Paul's birthplace, was located.

Acts 9:30 appears to represent Paul as sailing from Caesarea to Tarsus in Cilicia and as then passing from Cilicia into Syria. The order, therefore, in which the provinces are mentioned in the present passage is the order of their importance, not the order in which Paul traveled in them. Cilicia was in fact little more than an appendage of Syria; though named separately here, the two regions made up a single provincial district.

During this time of his ministry Paul had no direct and personal relations with the Christian community of Judea (in which Jerusalem was located). *I was*, he writes, *still unknown by face unto the churches of Judaea which were in Christ* (verse 22, asv). He therefore could not have been receiving guidance, instruction, or authority from that source. "The churches [congregations] of Judaea" taken literally would include the church at Jerusalem, but since Paul has just mentioned a brief visit to Jerusalem, it is likely that the reference here is to the churches outside of Jerusalem.

These Judean assemblies are described as being "in Christ." This phrase may have been used simply to distinguish them as *Christian* congregations, but some interpreters think there are larger implications. The Judean churches were "in Christ" in the sense that they were united to Him. He was the sphere of their being, and His will and service formed the very elements in which they lived and worked.

The apostle was known to these churches only by report. *They only heard it said, "He who once persecuted us is now preaching the faith he once tried to destroy"* (verse 23, rsv).

In the New Testament the word "faith" ordinarily denotes the trust which brings men into a saving relationship with God. Some interpreters understand it in that sense here. Burton, for instance, says this is the only way in which Paul ever uses the word. Others, however, interpret the word here to stand for the message of which faith in Christ is the central and distinctive element. Understood in this manner, faith is practically a synonym for the Gospel (cf. Acts 6:7; 13:8; Jude 3, 20). This, on the whole, is the better way of understanding the matter. To "preach" the faith, then, is to preach the Gospel.

Upon learning of Paul's conversion and Christian ministry, the Judean Christians who had once feared him as a persecutor found in him occasion and reason for praising God. Their joy formed a striking contrast to the attitude of the false teachers in Galatia. The latter, claiming to possess superior knowledge from Jerusalem, sought to discredit Paul. To silence them the apostle declares that the churches of Judea, those closest to the Twelve, *glorified God in me* (verse 24). The preposition denotes the sphere in which the action took place and perhaps also the foundation on which it rested. Taylor: "And they gave glory to God because of me." The glory which redounded to God from Paul's conversion wiped out much of the harm of his earlier opposition to the cause.

> When Jesus, here and there again,
>   His time of grace declares,
> That mercy count as thine own gain,
>   Which others find as theirs.

FOR FURTHER STUDY

1. Read Galatians in a translation you have not used before.
2. Read Luke's accounts of Paul's conversion in Acts 9:22, and 26.
3. Read an article on Judaism in a Bible dictionary. *The Zondervan Pictorial Bible Dictionary* and *The New Bible Dictionary* are both useful one-volume works.

CHAPTER 3

The Apostleship of Paul:

Acknowledged by the Jerusalem Apostles

(Galatians 2:1-10)

This paragraph, which continues the defense of Paul's apostolic authority, relates another occasion on which he had contact with the Jerusalem apostles. The emphasis, however, is somewhat different from that found in the preceding section. There Paul stressed significant details of his personal history which gave support to his contention that both his Gospel and his commission came from God, not men. The overall emphasis, therefore, was on his *independence* in relation to the Jerusalem apostles. Here the argument is taken a step beyond that, stressing not simply Paul's independence of the Twelve but also *their acquiescence* with him on a most important matter.

There has been considerable debate among the scholars as to the identity of the Jerusalem visit narrated here. Five such visits of the apostle are mentioned in Acts (9:26; 11:30; 15:2; 18:22; and 21:15), but only two of them (11:30; 15:2) could possibly have coincided with the visit recorded in the present passage[1]. The real question, then, is whether the visit of Galatians 2:1-10 is to be identified with the "famine visit" (Acts 11:30) or with the "council visit" (Acts 15).

Traditionally, the visit described in Galatians 2 has been identified with the "council visit" of Acts 15. The arguments supporting this view are both negative and positive. Negatively, its proponents say there is nothing in Acts 11:30 which gives even the slightest suggestion that the famine visit was concerned with the transactions mentioned in Galatians 2. Positively, they point to the remarkable similarities between the narrative of Acts 15 and that in Galatians 2. In both passagees Paul is accompanied by Barnabas and is seen contending with the Judaizers. Moreover, in both accounts it is affirmed that

---

[1] The visit mentioned in Galatians 1:18 is identical with the one mentioned in Acts 9:26, and the visits referred to in Acts 18:22 and 21:15 both came too late in the ministry of Paul to be identified with this visit.

35

Paul and Barnabas laid before the Jerusalem leaders a report of their preaching (Acts 15:12; Gal. 2:2). In addition, both accounts name Peter and James among the leading Jerusalem apostles. There are, to be sure, differences in the two accounts, but these differences do not mean the accounts are contradictory. They show rather that Acts 15 and Galatians 2 complement one another. Ridderbos explains that the two accounts reflect a difference in point of view. "In our letter the conference at Jerusalem is described in a polemical-apologetical argument; in Acts 15 it is described in a more impersonal and generally historical narrative" (pp. 78, 79). Hovey, in a similar vein, writes: "Luke's account is that of a historian desiring to present a sketch of the proceedings insofar as they affected all the churches; Paul's account is that of a man who desires to establish a single point, namely, that his teaching and authority were admitted to be Christian and apostolic by the greatest of the Twelve" (p. 24). In addition to the scholars cited above, this interpretation has been embraced by Lightfoot, Burton, Adeney, Williams, and others.

The view which in recent years has attracted increasing attention identifies the visit described by Paul with the famine visit (Acts 11:30). This theory, championed by Sir William Ramsay and held by many scholars today, has a number of things to commend it. At the same time it has, like the other theory, obvious weaknesses. The evidence, therfore, is not wholly satisfactory for either view, and one should avoid dogmatism in the matter. The present writer, with some hesitation, is inclined to follow those who identify this visit with the council visit of Acts 15. Fortunately, one's position on this matter will not appreciably affect his understanding of the argument. The point is that Paul had received nothing in the way of instruction or authority from the Jerusalem apostles, but on the contrary had been recognized by them as standing on a level with them.

The paragraph may be divided into three parts: verses 1 and 2 describe the occasion and circumstances of the visit; verses 3 through 5, which are really a parenthesis, refer to a specific incident which concerned Titus; versus 6 through 10, which resume the main subject of the paragraph, describe Paul's relations with the Jerusalem apostles.

I. The occasion and circumstances of the visit (2:1, 2).

The *time* of the visit is set out in verse 1a: *Then after the space of [i.e., a lapse of] fourteen years I went up again to Jerusalem* (asv). It is debated whether the "fourteen years" are to be dated from the time of Paul's conversion (1:15, 16) or from the time of his first visit to Jerusalem (1:18), which came three years after his conversion. Advocates of the former view tend to identify this incident with the famine visit (Acts 11:30ff) and argue that the apostle would not, in this context, omit mentioning any of his visits to Jerusalem. Proponents of the latter view, on the other hand, counter that Paul was not giving a complete listing of all his visits to Jerusalem but was simply listing those which had significance for his argument. These interpreters usually identify this event with the council visit of Acts 15. The matter is of considerable interest in establishing a chronology of Paul's life, but it is of small consequence for the exposition of his thought.

Paul's *companions* on this visit were Barnabas and Titus: *I went up . . . with Barnabas, taking Titus also with me* (verse 1b, ASV). In the early years of Paul's ministry, Barnabas was his closest associate. Robertson avers that Paul owed more to him than to any other man. It was Barnabas who befriended him when everyone else in Jerusalem was suspicious and afraid of him (Acts 9:27), and it was Barnabas who gave him an opportunity for a wider ministry in Antioch (Acts 11:25ff). Moreover, Barnabas was Paul's companion on the first missionary journey. The name of Barnabas would carry much weight with Paul's opponents, for no Hebrew Christian would question the orthodoxy of Barnabas. He was one of the most distinguished men in the Judaeo-Christian community.

Acts mentions Barnabas in connection with both the famine visit (Acts 11:30) and the council visit (Acts 15:2), but Titus is not named in either account. However, Acts 15:2 does state that "certain other" members of the church were sent along with Paul and Barnabas. The reference to Titus in the present passage, therefore, in no way contradicts the narrative in Acts 15. Titus was a *Greek* (verse 3); that is, he was a Gentile and of pagan origin. He had not been circumcised (verse 3), and perhaps that is the very reason for Paul's bringing him to Jerusalem. Numerous references to Titus are found in 2 Corinthians (2:13; 7:6, 13ff; 8:6, 16, 23; 12:18) and in the Pastoral Epistles (2 Tim. 4:10; Titus 1:4, etc.), but he is not named at all in the Book of Acts. The manner in which his name is introduced into the passage before us shows that Paul assumed full responsibility for his presence with him at Jerusalem.

Paul next explains that he went up to Jerusalem *by [in accordance with a] revelation* (verse 2). This means that the trip was not undertaken on his own initiative, nor was it solely because of the urging of the church at Antioch (as one might conclude from reading Acts

15:2). It came about as the result of a revelation given by God. Precisely how this revelation came, we are not told. It could have been made to Paul in person, or it could have been given through the Holy Spirit to the church, and through the church to Paul. The important thing is that Paul was conscious of divine guidance and was convinced that it was God's will for him to go to Jerusalem. The council which the apostle called for at Jerusalem was to determine for all time the question of whether Christians were required to observe the Mosaic law. This was the very issue which had been revived by Paul's opponents in the Galatian churches.

The *purpose* of this trip was to make known to the Jerusalem church Paul's message. Accordingly he writes: *I . . . communicated unto them [i.e., the church generally] that gospel which I preach among the Gentiles* (verse 2). "Communicated" translates a Greek word which means "to present" or "to lay before." What Paul laid before the Jerusalem brethren is designated as "the gospel which I preach among the Gentiles." The questions at issue between Paul and his opponents — at the time of the Council as well as at the time of writing this letter — concerned the heart of the Gospel, that is, the significance of Christ's work and the terms of salvation.

Observe the present tense of the verb "preach." Paul affirms that the Gospel which he proclaimed at the time of the Council (and which received its sanction) is the same Gospel which he still preaches. Over the years, there had been no change in the essence of his message. He did not, as some of his opponents may have suggested, alter his message to suit his hearers. If "a different gospel" was being preached to the Galatians, it was the false teachers who were doing it, not Paul.

"Among the Gentiles" suggests that Paul thought of his apostleship not simply as a ministry to *Gentile people* but as a ministry to *all people* in Gentile lands. That is to say, he preached not only to Gentiles but also to the Jews who happened to live in Gentile lands.

Verse 2 seems to suggest that in addition to the public meeting with the church (verse 2b), there was a private meeting with the recognized leaders: *them which were of reputation* (verse 2c; cf. verses 6, 9). The persons so described were probably those whom Luke designates as "apostles and elders" (Acts 15:2, 4, 6). Paul's expression is a term of honor denoting men of influence in the Christian community at Jerusalem. Burton renders it "men of eminence" (p. 71); Moffatt, "the authorities"; Weymouth, "the leaders of the Church." In verse 9 they (or at least the three principal ones) are identified as James,

Cephas, and John. This private meeting, writes Lightfoot, "was a wise precaution to avoid misunderstanding: the public conference was a matter of necessity to obtain recognition of the freedom of the Gentile churches" (p. 103).

Paul's fear was that the opposition of the Jerusalem church — especially opposition of the leaders in that church — might render ineffectual both his past and future work in behalf of the Gentiles. If he could not convince the leaders in Jerusalem of the legitimacy of his message and commission, he would be like a runner who, in spite of all his efforts, failed to receive the prize of victory. As he puts it, "I laid . . . the gospel which I preach . . . before them who were of repute, *lest by any means I should be running, or had run, in vain*" (verse 2, asv).

The ground of Paul's apprehension was in no way doubt concerning the truth of his Gospel. He was not unsure of himself nor of what he preached. He was convinced, however, that the disapproval of his work by the Jerusalem apostles would to a great extent neutralize his efforts in behalf of the Gentiles, however true his message might be. Pfleiderer explains the situation as follows:

> We may imagine in what a painful situation the apostle . . . found himself. If the party zealous for the Law should be successful with their demand that the believing Gentiles must by circumcision submit to the Jewish Law, and if it should be confirmed that in this demand they really had the parent church, together with the apostles, on their side, the mission to the Gentiles was at an end, and the life-work of the apostle to the heathen was hopeless. . . . If Paul had, on the other hand, simply ignored the demands of the Judaizers, without coming to any understanding with the earlier apostles and obtaining their sanction of his Gentile mission, with its freedom from the Law, he would have severed the connection of his heathen churches with the parent church, and the Gentile church, thus isolated from the very first and degraded to a sect, would hardly have been able long to maintain its existence. The continuance or the destruction of his life-work depended, therefore, now, to Paul's mind, on whether he succeeded in obtaining from the parent church and its leaders the acknowledgment of their Christian fellowship for his gentile Christians as such (quoted by Hovey, p. 25).

Burton explains that Paul's "unshaken confidence in the divine origin and the truth of his own gospel did not prevent his seeing that the rupture which would result from a refusal of the pillar apostles . . . to recognize the legitimacy of his mission and gospel . . . would be disastrous alike to the Jewish and the Gentile parties which would thus be created" (p. 73).

II. THE CASE OF TITUS (2:3-5).

This entire passage is inserted parenthetically, but it makes a significant contribution to the apostle's argument. Cole, calling attention to the irregularity of its grammar and the compressed character of its thought, describes it as "notoriously difficult" (p. 63). The incident occurred within the context of the Jerusalem Conference and highlighted the central issues of that historic event.

The meaning of verse 3, which in both KJV and ASV is rather obscure, is clearly expressed by Norlie: *But they did not even compel my companion Titus, who was a Greek, to be circumcised.* That is, neither the church generally nor the leaders of the church ("those who were of repute") insisted that so well-known a Gentile as Titus be circumcised. The import of the entire statement is that both the church and its leaders were in agreement with Paul in the matter of circumcision. Had they thought it was necessary for salvation they would surely have urged Titus to submit to the rite.

Verses 4 and 5 explain that there were some in Jerusalem who did insist that Titus be circumcised. They doubtless reminded Paul that on an earlier occasion he had had Timothy circumcised (Acts 16:3). The two cases, however, were not parallel. Timothy was the son of a Jewess, and his submission to circumcision was a practical compromise to make for more effective ministry among his own people. Titus, on the other hand, was wholly Gentile, and a vital principle was at stake in his case. He was, in a sense, the very embodiment of the issue under consideration, and concession to the Judaizers in reference to him would have undermined Paul's whole position. The apostle therefore refused to give in to the demands of the circumcisionists. And in his position he had the support of the church and its pillar apostles (verse 3).

Verse 4 may be seen as giving the source of the controversy about Titus. The verse is admittedly obscure, and no explanation of it is entirely satisfactory. The RSV interprets it as an anacolution (an incomplete sentence). Some interpreters (e.g. MacKenzie) see it as giving the reason for Paul's private consultation (verse 2) with the "men of repute." Others (e.g. Williams) think it gives the reason why Titus was not circumcised. It may be best to interpret it as "an appositive amplifier" (Ridderbos, p. 83) of the thought of verse 3. There it is asserted that the leading figures at Jerusalem did not require Titus to be circumcised. Here we are told that there nevertheless were some in Jerusalem who demanded it. Norlie: *This question came up because of some false brethren, etc.*

These opponents of Paul are designated as "brethren" because they *claimed* to be Christians; they are called "false" brethren because Paul did not think they were *real* Christians. (Compare 2 Cor. 11:26, the only other New Testament passage in which the expression occurs.)

Three other things are said about the false brethren: First, they were *privily* [secretly] brought in (ASV) — smuggled in, we might say. This expression, which is further evidence that the men involved were false brethren, marks them as alien to the Christian company. The passive force of the word suggests that they were either "planted" in the church by outsiders (i.e., unbelieving Jews) or were smuggled into the Christian community by persons within the church. (The Greek word was used by one of the ancient writers to denote the treacherous introduction of foreign enemies into a city by a faction within the city.) We are not told where the infiltration occurred. Guthrie conjectures that it was at Antioch (cf. Acts 15:1).

Second, they *came in privily to spy out our liberty which we have in Christ Jesus.* That is to say, they were seeking evidence of disregard for the Mosaic law on the part of Jewish Christians. Guthrie comments: "They were acting like intelligence agents building up a case against slackness over Jewish ritual requirements" (p. 80). The Greek word for "to spy out" simply means "to examine carefully," but it has here a connotation of hostile intent. The suggestion is that of searching out with a view of overthrowing. What they wanted to overthrow is defined as "our liberty which we have in Christ Jesus." This phrase, which sums up better than any other the fundamental theme of the letter (cf. 4:22-31; 5:1, 13), has reference to the Christian's freedom from the ritual requirements of the Mosaic law.

Third, the ultimate purpose of the false brethren was to *bring us into bondage [to the law]* (ASV). That is to say, they hoped to enforce the Jewish law on Paul and all of his Gentile converts. The apostle interpreted this as an attempt to reduce the Christian community to a state of spiritual slavery. Paul is careful to explain this because his opponents in Galatia, like the false brethren at the Jerusalem Conference, sought to require circumcision of all Gentile believers. Paul implies that for the Galatians to give in to them would mean the loss of their freedom.

Verse 5a asserts Paul's resolute opposition to the false brethren: *to whom we gave place in the way of subjection, no, not for an hour* (ASV). The language suggests that Paul never even entertained the thought of submitting to the demand for Titus' circumcision. "Subjection", which literally reads *"the* subjection," means "the subjection (submission) which they (the Judaizers) required."

The words "not for an hour" mean "not even for a short time." In English we might convey it by the words "not for a moment." Moffatt: "But we refused to yield for a single instant."

The purpose of Paul's refusal to yield is stated in the words *that the truth of the gospel might continue with you* (verse 5b). Had his opponents persuaded him to yield to their position, the Gentiles would have been robbed of the true Gospel and left with a false gospel. "The truth of the gospel" is the truth *belonging to* the Gospel, or perhaps the truth which *is* the Gospel. Sensing that the integrity of the Gospel was at stake, Paul adamantly stood his ground and won the victory.

"With you" suggests the far-reaching effects of the struggle in Jerusalem. In championing the case of Titus Paul felt that he was fighting a battle for the whole Christian community. The victory won at Jerusalem was therefore, for all practical purposes, a victory for the Galatian Christians. Coad comments that "the very confusion, almost incoherence, of [Paul's] language in this passage . . . is evidence of what that struggle had cost him, and of how deeply it stirred him to find himself fighting the same battle yet again. Today, looking back at the long history of the Church, we can realize something of the immensity of the issues for which he contended, and can admire again the largeness and penetration of his vision" (p. 449).

III. PAUL AND THE PILLAR APOSTLES (2:6-10).

These verses form one long sentence interrupted twice by parentheses (verses 6b, 8) and once broken off and begun anew in altered form (verse 6c). Many thoughts converge, but the principal subject is the agreement reached in Jerusalem between Paul and Barnabas and the three leading apostles. The latter, we are told, recognized the special grace which had been destowed on Paul and Barnabas, equipping them for work among the Gentiles. They therefore gave them the right hands of fellowship, acknowledging that they were all partners in a common cause.

Verses 6-10 are really a continuation of the thought of verse 2, the intervening verses (3-5) being parenthetical. Verse 2 makes mention of the private meeting with the men of repute. These verses (6-10) tell of the outcome of that meeting. It is summed up in three assertions.

1. *They . . . imparted nothing to me* is the essential statement of

verse 6. The meaning is that Paul learned nothing from the men of repute that he did not already know and gained no authority from them that he did not already possess.

The verse has three distinct parts. It begins as though the apostle were going to write "And from those who were reputed to be something nothing was imparted to me." However, he turns away from completing the thought in order to make a parenthetical comment concerning "those who were reputed to be something." The parenthesis, which is the second part of the verse, reads: *whatsoever they were, it maketh no matter to me: God accepteth no man's person* (verse 6b). This may mean, "Call them what you will, it matters not to me." Some scholars think the stress is on "were," the reference being to the supposed advantage which the Jerusalem apostles possessed over Paul by their association with the Lord during His earthly ministry. Paul's comment implies that this advantage of the senior apostles had been thrown up to him as a mark of his inferiority. The apostle contends that things of this sort are of no concern to him, that they have no real significance. He justifies his statement by declaring that "God accepteth no man's person" — literally, "God does not accept the face of man." That is, God does not base His judgment and action on external considerations. Worldly distinctions do not at all sway Him. The RSV renders it, "God shows no partiality"; TCNT, "God does not recognize human distinctions"; Phillips, "God is not impressed with a man's office."

The third part of the verse (*for they who seemed to be somewhat,* etc., verse 6c) resumes the thought begun at the start of verse 6. Evidently what Paul intended to say there, he now says in this slightly altered form. The principal apostles, he declares, *imparted nothing to me* (ASV). The emphasis is on the words "to me," the suggestion being that though Paul added much to their understanding of the Gospel they had nothing to impart to him.

2. *They gave to me and Barnabas the right hands of fellowship* (verse 9). This, the main statement of verses 7-9, asserts the positive side of Paul's relationship with Peter, James, and John. Instead of correcting his doctrine or of conveying to him any new truth, the pillar apostles conceded the truth of his Gospel, recognized the genuineness of his commission, and acknowledged him as an equal. Two circumstances led to this recognition: First, *they [Peter, James, and John] saw that the gospel of the uncircumcision was committed unto me [Paul], [just] as the gospel of the circumcision was unto Peter . . .* (verse 7). The "seeing" is to be taken in the sense of mental and

spiritual perception. What they perceived was the divine source of
Paul's ministry. God had obviously set him apart for a special work
among the Gentiles, just as Peter had been given a special ministry
among the Jews. The same God who had commissioned Peter to
preach to the one commissioned Paul to preach to the other. Both
were accountable only to God.

"The gospel of the uncircumcision" is the gospel for Gentiles; "the
gospel of the circumcision" is the gospel for Jews. The difference is
not one of content, but of the persons for whom the message is intended. The idea of two gospels different in content is utterly foreign
to this epistle — and indeed to the entire New Testament.

Verse 8, a parenthesis, is an expansion upon the thought of verse 7.
The latter verse has traced the commissions of Peter and Paul to one
source. Verse 8 affirms that the God who commissioned the two men
empowered both of them for their work and sealed their ministries
with fruit. *For he that wrought for Peter unto the apostleship of the
circumcision wrought for me also unto the Gentiles* (ASV). "Wrought"
renders a Greek verb from which we get the word "energize." A word
frequently found in Paul, it speaks mainly of the inward endowment
for the work of ministry. Moffatt uses the word "equipped"; TCNT,
"gave . . . power." In this context it may also embrace the outward
signs which sealed the ministry (cf. Phillips' rendering). "Apostleship,"
a word found elsewhere in the New Testament only in Acts 1:25;
Romans 1:5; and 1 Corinthians 9:2, here has reference not to the
commission, "but to the carrying out of it, the execution" (Ridderbos,
p. 89). The RSV translates it "mission." Apostleship "of the circumcision" therefore means something like ministry (mission) to the
Jews. "In Peter" and "in me" mean, respectively, "on Peter's behalf,"
"on my behalf."

Verse 9, which resumes the thought of verse 7, defines the second
circumstance which led to the recognition of Paul: *James, Cephas,
and John . . . perceived the grace that was given unto me.* The three
men, who have been alluded to in verse 2 ("them which were of
reputation") and in verse 6 ("those who seemed to be somewhat") are
now for the first time named. The listing of the name of James first
probably reflects both his prominence in the Jerusalem church and
the force of his influence in the settlement of the question under consideration (cf. Acts 15). It should be pointed out that this "James"
was the brother of our Lord, not James, the brother of John. The
latter already had suffered martyrdom by the time of the incident
recorded here.

"Who were reputed to be pillars" reflects the language of Paul's opponents, who might habitually have referred to these three men as the "pillars" of the church. Some scholars think Paul was disputing this characterization, implying that they were not really pillars, but only "reputed" to be such. Guthrie concedes the possibility of some tension between Paul and the Jerusalem apostles, but doubts that in a context stressing fellowship with them he would have said anything to imply opposition. "It is much more probable, therefore, that Paul is referring to the reputation of James, Cephas, and John in order to bring out more forcefully the significance of the agreement with them. It was as if Paul had said that even the acknowledged 'pillars' were prepared to have fellowship with him" (p. 85).

The giving of "right hands" was the outward token of a mutual compact or agreement. Williams thinks it probably was "a public manifestation of agreement" (p. 41). TCNT: "openly acknowledged." The adding of the phrase "of fellowship" marks the agreement as one of partnership. Paul and Barnabas were to go "unto the heathen" (that is, to the Gentiles) and James, Cephas, and John "unto the circumcision" (that is, to the Jews).

Burton appropriately comments that the whole of verse 9 "marks the complete victory of the apostle on this memorable occasion" (p. 97).

3. They requested *that we should remember the poor* (verse 10). This is stated as a kind of addendum to the agreement reached. The tense of the verb, which expresses continued action, attests that the course of action referred to was one which already had been followed.

Paul adds: *which very thing I was also zealous to do* (verse 10b, ASV). The verb used in this clause means "to do with eagerness" or "to make diligent effort (to do a thing)." The change from first person plural ("that *we* should remember") to first person singular ("*I* also was zealous") reflects the parting of Paul and Barnabas before the start of the second missionary journey. Paul, being no longer intimately associated with the work of Barnabas, speaks only for himself.

To sum up, Paul has proved two things in this passage: (1) He and the Jerusalem apostles were in total agreement; and (2) a cordial relationship existed between them.

For Further Study

1. Read Acts 15.
2. Read articles on Titus, Barnabas, James, Cephas (Peter), and John.
3. Read articles on the "Judaizers" and "Circumcision."

CHAPTER 4

The Apostleship of Paul:

Asserted in the Clash With Peter

(Galatians 2:11-21)

To this point Paul has advanced two arguments, both drawn from his personal life, to show that his apostleship is as valid as that of the Twelve. He began (1:11-24) with a resume of his conversion and his early ministry, the circumstances of which pointed up his *independence* of the Twelve. This was followed (2:1-10) with a discussion of the Jerusalem Conference, where Paul was *recognized as an equal* by the other apostles.

After Paul and Barnabas had successfully defended their position in the momentous Conference at Jerusalem, the two men returned to Antioch. Their report to the church at Antioch must have cheered the Gentile believers there, and we can imagine that for some time all went well. Eventually, however, another situation arose which posed a serious threat to the unity and fellowship of the church. Peter, the leading Jerusalem apostle, was a contributor to this new outbreak of factionalism, and Paul as a matter of principle felt compelled to resist him. This event is described in 2:11-21, and the discussion of it constitutes a third and final line of evidence presented by Paul in support of the validity of his apostolic authority. The incident shows conclusively that he in no way acted in subordination to the Jerusalem apostles. Nor did he acknowledge any dependence on them, for here he set his own authority over against that of one of the pillars of the Jerusalem church. Burton calls this "one of the most significant incidents of the whole series from the point of view of [Paul's] independence of the apostles" (p. 100).

We are not told when this confrontation between Paul and Peter took place, and the Book of Acts makes no mention of it. Obviously, it followed the event recorded in 2:1-10, but how much time elapsed between the two we cannot know. Some interpreters think it was several years. Findlay, for example, suggests that it came in the in-

46

terval between the second and third missionary journeys. Others
(Lightfoot, for instance) feel that the incident occurred soon after
the Conference. It seems unlikely, however, that the circumcision
party could have recouped its forces and increased its influence so
soon.

The passage under consideration falls naturally into two divisions.
The first (verses 11-14a) describes the confrontation with Peter; the
second (verses 14b-21) gives the essence of Paul's argument at the
time.

I. THE CONFRONTATION WITH PETER (2:11-14a).

Findlay thinks this occurrence was the second stage of Paul's conflict with legalism. The utterances of Peter and James at the Jerusalem
Conference, and the letter addressed therefrom to the Gentile churches,
made the Judaizers take a different approach. To be sure, they did not
surrender; they merely "made a change of front," adopting "a subtler
and seemingly more moderate view" (Findlay, p. 130). They now began to teach that legal observances opened up privileges to believers
which were denied to those who refused to be burdened by the ceremonial law, arguing that circumcision was a divine ordinance which
must have its benefit. Findlay supposes their explanation to have run
as follows:

> God has given to Israel an indefeasible preeminence in His king-
> dom. Law-keeping children of Abraham enter the new Covenant on
> a higher footing than "sinners of the Gentiles": they are still the elect
> race, the holy nation. If the Gentiles wish to share with them, they
> must add to their faith circumcision, they must complete their imper-
> fect righteousness by legal sanctity. So they might hope to enter on
> the full heritage of the sons of Abraham; they would be brought into
> communion with the first Apostles and the Brother of the Lord; they
> would be admitted to the inner circle of the kingdom of God. The
> new Legalists sought, in fact, to impose Jewish law on Gentile Chris-
> tianity. They no longer refused all share in Christ to the uncircum-
> cised; they offered them a larger share (pp. 130, 131).

Legalists, they taught, were a spiritual aristocracy within the church.
It was this aspect of the Judaizing heresy which Paul in Galatians was
combating, and which Peter had on one occasion been led to coun-
tenance. For this, Paul sharply rebuked the reputed leader of the
Twelve.

1. *A summary statement* (verse 11). Verse 11 states in summary
fashion the essential facts of the confrontation between these two great
men. *But when Peter was come to Antioch, I withstood him to the*

face, because he was to be blamed. From this statement we may learn three things about this conflict. First, it occurred in "Antioch." Two cities connected with the ministry of Paul bore this name – one in Pisidia and the other, which was the more famous, in Syria. The latter was the center of Gentile Christianity and doubtless the city referred to in the present verse. There is no way of knowing when Peter arrived there. We are assuming that it was somtime near the close of Paul's second missionary journey. Burton thinks the passage implies that Paul was not present when Peter first arrived; he conjectures that a considerable series of events must have occurred before the encounter between the two men.

Second, the conflict involved a face to face confrontation: "I resisted him to the face" (ASV). The verb employed suggests a response to an attack and implies that Paul interpreted Peter's conduct, however unintentional, to be an attack on the position which he had championed at Antioch. "To the face" is, for the sake of emphasis, placed first in the Greek clause. The entire expression accords with all that is known of Paul's conviction, courage, and openness. Peter was one of the chief apostles and was highly regarded by the Christian community. It was therefore not easy to oppose him in the fashion indicated here.

Third, the reason for Paul's opposition is stated in the words "because he stood condemned" (ASV). That is to say, Peter had acted inconsistently (as will be shown in the following verses) and "stood condemned" by his own conduct even before Paul challenged him. "The condemnation," writes Lightfoot, "is not the verdict of the bystanders, but the verdict of the act itself" (p. 111). Perhaps it could be rendered "because he was guilty." Rendall, who thinks the versions are in error in translating this as a causal clause, prefers to translate it as declarative: "I withstood him [Peter], saying that he had condemned himself" (p. 162).

2. *Peter's conduct* (verses 12, 13). Verses 12 and 13 describe Peter's conduct on this occasion, telling what he did when he first arrived in Antioch (verse 12a), what he did after the arrival of emissaries from Jerusalem (verse 12b), and the effect of his behavior upon his associates (verse 13).

When Peter first came to Antioch his custom was to *eat with the Gentiles* (verse 12a). The reference is to table fellowship in the homes of Gentiles. Rabbinic regulations on this matter were very strict, but Peter's experience in the Cornelius incident had taught him that a Jew was not defiled by social contacts with Gentiles. He therefore, upon arriving in Antioch, moved freely among the Gentile believers and gladly shared the hospitality of their homes.

This was *before certain men came from James* (verse 12, RSV). This may mean that the persons so described were sent by James to Antioch (for what purpose we are not told), or it may mean simply that they came from the church in Jerusalem, of which James was the pastor. At any rate, it is doubtful that they were sent by James to deal with the relationships between Jews and Gentiles. Williams thinks they may have been on a tour to solicit alms for the poor.

The context implies that these emissaries from Jerusalem were shocked to see Jewish and Gentile believers enjoying fellowship with one another and sharing meals at the same table. Being thorough-going legalists, they insisted that Jews should avoid social contacts with uncircumcised Gentiles.

After these men from James came, Peter *withdrew and separated himself* (verse 12b). The words "withdrew" and "separated" render a tense construction which has inceptive force. The TCNT brings this out in translation: "he *began* to withdraw," etc. (italics mine). This suggests that the action was gradual and possibly reluctant. The word for "withdrew" (ASV: "he drew back") "suggests an unobtrusive retreat" (Ridderbos, p. 96). Burton says it was used in classical Greek of the withdrawal of troops and "suggests a retreat from motives of caution" (p. 107). The Greek word is used in the Septuagint as a semi-technical term for separation from unclean things.

The last part of verse 12 explains the reason for Peter's action: *fearing them which were of the circumcision.* That is, he feared that the Jews would censure his conduct and cause him to lose the good will of the Jewish Christians in Jerusalem. Chrysostom interpreted it to mean that Peter feared not for himself but for the Jewish believers, lest they should be offended and renounce the faith. This, however, can hardly be the meaning. Some commentaries take "them which were of the circumcision" as a designation not simply of those who insisted on circumcision (the Judaizers) but of Jewish believers generally. Weymouth and RSV, however, take it in the first sense, "the circumcision party."

Verse 13 gives evidence of the tremendous effect of Peter's influence. Not only did *the rest of the Jews* dissemble (play the hypocrite) with him, but *even Barnabas was carried away with their dissimulation* (verse 13, ASV). There is no indication here that Peter deliberately solicited the other Christian Jews of Antioch to take this course. He himself had doubtless yielded to the pressures from the Jerusalem brethren with great reluctance. But the fact that he yielded at all must have carried much weight with lesser men in Antioch.

Just how strong the Judaizing tendency was at this time is clearly brought out in the reference to Barnabas. "Even" (cf. ASV) the man who was the companion of Paul and one of the most respected leaders of the entire Christian movement "was carried away with" their hypocrisy. (The voice of the verb is significant, implying that Barnabas did not play an active role but was for the moment "swept off his balance" [Guthrie, p. 88]. Lightfoot comments that the word represents the dissimulation at Antioch as "a flood which swept everything away with it" [p. 113].) Paul's language suggests the high regard in which he held Barnabas and the surprise and disappointment which were his when his friend of many years yielded to the pressures of the Judaizing Christians.

The word "dissimulation" ("insincerity," RSV), from which we get "hypocrisy," ordinarily denotes the concealment of one's real character and feelings so as to appear to be something different. In this case Peter and "the other Jews" (i.e., Jewish members of the church at Antioch) pretended that their action stemmed from loyalty to the Mosaic law, but it was in reality prompted by fear. Paul implies that there had been no real change of conviction; their conduct was simply a betrayal of true convictions.

3. *Paul's reaction* (verse 14). Verse 14 explains that Paul was shocked to see that Peter, Barnabas, and other Jewish Christians of Antioch *walked not uprightly according to the truth of the gospel* (verse 14a). Knox renders it, "they were not following the true path of the gospel"; NEB, "their conduct did not square with the truth of the Gospel." A literal rendering of the Greek suggests that they were *not pursuing a straight course* in reference to the truth of the Gospel. The root of the verb means "straight-footed"; from this the verb itself came to mean to walk straightforwardly, with the intimation that one leaves a straight path for others to follow. (On the phrase "the truth of the gospel" compare the statement in 2:5. Here it denotes the standard from which Peter and his companions had deviated.)

I said unto Peter before them all emphasizes the public nature of the rebuke. It probably was administered in this fashion because of the public character of Peter's offense; only by an equally public rebuke could its baneful influence be counteracted. In addition, such public rebuke would weigh upon the consciences of those who had dissembled with Peter. By stressing this aspect of the rebuke Paul conveys to his readers that he in confrontation with the chief of the apostles did more than just hold his own.

B. THE ADDRESS TO PETER (1:14b-21).

The substance of Paul's rebuke to Peter is given in these verses. They begin with a quotation of some of the actual words used on the occasion (verse 14b), and this is followed by a sort of summary which gives the general drift of the argument by which Paul supported his case (verses 15-21). Thus what begins as an argument addressed to Peter passes over into one addressed to the Galatians. The original speech was surely much longer and may well have been varied by conversational interruptions. Much of what is recorded here "reads rather like a meditative working up of what was said in the heat of controversy with later reflection" (Adeney, p. 282). The whole paragraph serves as a transition statement preparing us for the apostle's defense of his Gospel in chapters 3 and 4.

Paul begins by pointing up the inconsistency of Peter's conduct: *If thou, being a Jew, livest after the manner of Gentiles, and not as do the Jews, why compellest thou the Gentiles to live as do the Jews?* (verse 14b). "Being a Jew" means something like "being a Jew to begin with." In other words, Peter was born and bred a Jew. The verb for "livest" is present tense, suggesting that the pattern and habit of Peter's life prior to this incident was like that of non-Jews. That is to say, he accepted their customs in reference to food and associated with them as equals in the Gospel. Paul takes it for granted that it was right and proper for him to do so.

"Why compellest thou [RSV: 'how can you compel'] the Gentiles to live as do the Jews" shows that Paul interpreted Peter's act as an inconsistency having far-reaching effects upon Gentile Christians. For all practical purposes it amounted to an attempt to coerce them into observing Jewish customs. "The force of his example," writes Lightfoot, "became a species of compulsion" (p. 114). Such was probably not the intention of Peter, but it was precisely what the Judaizers wanted. The ambiguity of Peter's conduct played right into their hands.

Paul's words were bold and severe, and it is indicative of the bigness of Peter that he could take such public rebuke in a spirit of humility and meekness. There is no indication here or in any of the writings of Peter that he tried to defend his conduct, nor that he held this public rebuke against Paul in later years.

In verse 15 Paul turns from the second person singular pronoun ("thou") to the first person plural ("we"). In so doing, he associates himself with Peter and expresses the whole argument in a more courteous and conciliatory manner. Hunter calls attention to "the identity of opinion" which is here assumed between Peter and Paul. "It is taken for granted, not only that Peter is a Christian but that he is a Christian of a *Pauline* type. We sometimes suppose that the doctrine of 'justification by faith' is Paul's own contribution to the gospel. Here Paul makes it quite clear that it was something which all Christians held" (p. 23).

The gist of verses 15 and 16 is as follows: "You and I, Peter, are Jews by nature and not pagan-born sinners; yet because we know [as a matter of principle] that there is only one way to get right with God (and that is through trusting Jesus) even we have believed in Christ Jesus in order that we might be justified by faith in Christ and not by works of law." The main statement of this involved sentence is found in the words "even we have believed in Christ Jesus." This is modified by a concessive clause ("we being Jews by nature," etc., ASV), a casual clause ("yet knowing that a man is not justified by the works of the law," etc., ASV), a purpose clause ("that we might be justified by the faith of Christ," etc.), and a clause confirming the entire statement ("for by the works of the law," etc.).

"Jews by nature" was Paul's way of saying that he and Peter were born Jews and by virtue of this fact possessed all the advantages of knowledge of the law and opportunity of achieving righteousness through it. "Sinners of the Gentiles" does not designate a particular group of people among the Gentiles; it rather denotes Gentiles in general. The Jews thought of all of them as "sinners" and sometimes used the words interchangeably. Paul simply adopts here the current Jewish way of thinking and speaking. Elsewhere he calls Gentiles "lawless" (Rom. 2:12) and "without God" (Eph. 2:12). Sanday takes the words in the present passage to mean "of Gentile parentage (and therefore) sinners" (p. 437).

Verse 16 shows that the Jew, in spite of his superior privileges, was really in no better position than the Gentile. On his own, neither can achieve right standing before God. The first part of the verse states the principle; the second part recounts the experience of Paul and Peter (and other Jewish believers); the final clause of the verse gives a confirmation of the inadequacy of law by a reference to Old Testament scripture.

The word translated *justified* means "to be declared righteous," "to be treated as righteous," that is, to be accounted by God as acceptable to him. It is one of the great words of the Pauline letters, and it is imperative that one grasp its meaning if he is to interpret Paul correctly. It is a particularly important word for this present epistle.

Works of the law are deeds of obedience to the Mosaic law performed with an expectation of meriting and securing a right standing with God. The Judaizers believed in justification by faith to a certain extent, but they argued that works of the law had to be performed to make faith truly effectual. Against this Paul teaches that justification comes *through faith in Jesus Christ* (ASV). It is assumed that the grounds for justification are in Jesus Christ and what He has done for us; faith is said to be the means by which the benefits of His work are communicated to us. The emphasis is on the fact that justification comes not from something within ourselves but from our relationship with Christ.

"Faith," which is another of the central concepts of the writings of Paul, denotes trust and commitment.

"Even we have believed in Jesus Christ," as stated above, is the central affirmation of verses 15 and 16. The pronoun ("we") is emphatic, and added emphasis is given by the use of the particle "even." "In Jesus Christ" translates a construction which conveys the thought of entrusting one's self to Christ.

The last clause of verse 16 is added to confirm by the authority of Scripture the declaration that justification is through faith and not through the works of the law. The words are apparently taken from Psalm 143:2. Paul's statement, though not an exact quotation, is a correct interpretation of the essential meaning. The Psalm affirms in the most general way that no human being can be justified before God. Paul, by adding the words "by works of the law," interprets the psalm to mean that no man can be justified before God if judged on a basis of merit.

The thought of verses 17 and 18 is particularly difficult to follow. Some interpret it as follows: "You and I, Peter, in order to be justified, found it necessary to renounce the law and put our faith solely in Christ. We thus in a sense sank to the level of Gentiles, in fact became 'sinners.' Your action, Peter, in withdrawing from the Gentiles implies that we acted wrongly in our renunciation of the law. If you are correct in this, then we have made Christ a promoter of sin because it was He who led us to abandon the law, and it was He who inspired you to associate with the Gentiles. The very thought is abhorrent. Christ cannot possibly be responsible for sin. No, the sin is not in abandoning the law, but in going back to the law once it has been abandoned. Only in this way do we convict ourselves of transgression." Others see Paul's words as an answer to the charge that this doctrine of justification by faith alone encourages sin (cf. Rom. 6:1, 15). Guthrie states it succinctly: "The thought is that if the process of justification leads men into sin, this would make Christ an agent for producing sin, which would be clearly opposed to the nature of Christ. Paul strongly repudiates such an idea" (p. 91).

The statement of verses 17 and 18 is confirmed by verse 19. *For I through the law am dead to the law, that I might live unto God.* Lightfoot thinks the first pronoun (which is emphatic) does not mean "I, Paul" as distinguished from others, but rather "I, Paul, the natural man, the slave of the old covenant" p. 117). Those interpreters are on sounder ground, however, who explain it to mean "I for my own part." That is, "Whatever may be the experience of others, this is my experience." The phrase "through the law" is also emphatic, the point being that it was the law itself which drove Paul to cease to live in that realm in which law was the ruling principle. Ridderbos explains it as follows: "The law has put him to death for its service, whipped him to death, so to speak, by its demands. . . . All it can do is to demand, to forbid, to judge, and to condemn. So it is that man dies through the law: he is beaten to death by it and falls into God's judgment" (p. 104). Interpreted in this manner, the thought is similar to that of Romans 7. There Paul teaches that the law is holy and just and good but is powerless to save. Indeed, it condemns those who are under it for their inability to fulfill its requirements. Thus, under the law one is brought to the point of despair. His only hope is to throw off the bondage of the law and seek deliverance elsewhere — in Christ.

This death to the law took place at the time of Paul's conversion. The end result of it was that he came to "live unto God" (verse 19b). The language suggests a "God-directed, God-consecrated life" (Ridderbos, p. 103), "life under the control of God and for the honour of God" (Guthrie, p. 93).

Verse 20 describes the new life into which Paul came when he renounced the law and turned to Christ. It was in essence a life of identification with Christ, both in death and in resurrection. The former, identification in death, is expressed by the opening words: *I have been crucified with Christ* (asv). Believers, by virtue of their corporate union with Christ, were included in his death (cf. Rom. 6:6). What he experienced, they experienced. This may be seen as yet another reason why the law has no claim on Paul. Phillips: "As far as the Law is concerned I may consider that I died on the cross with Christ." The tense of the verb (perfect) speaks of an act accomplished at some point in the past but having abiding results.

But Paul's Christian experience involved not simply an identification with Christ in death; it was also an identification with him in life. *I have been crucified with Christ; and it is no longer I that live, but Christ liveth in me* (verse 20a, ASV). The sense is that Paul no longer thinks of himself as having a separate existence from Christ. Christ has become the source, the aim, and the motivating principle of all that he does (cf. Phil. 1:21). "As in the old days the law had filled his horizon and dominated his thought-life, so now it is Christ. Christ is the sole meaning of life for him now; every moment is passed in conscious dependence on Him" (Cole, p. 83).

In the words *and that life which I now live [that is, after having died with Christ] in the flesh I live in faith, the faith which is in the Son of God, who loved me, and gave himself up for me* (verse 20b, ASV), Paul describes life in Christ more precisely. Essentially it is a life of faith in contrast to the life of law which was his before conversion. And it is a certain kind of faith, one that is directed toward and centers in the Son of God.

Verse 21 is a sort of summary of the whole argument. *I do not frustrate the grace of God: for if righteousness come by the law, then Christ is dead in vain.* The word rendered "frustrate" means "to set aside," "to reject." The ASV has "make void." Several translations (e.g., Weymouth, RSV, NEB) use "nullify."

Some interpreters think Paul was here answering an accusation made against him by his opponents, namely, that his teaching in reference to the law rendered null and void the special grace of God to Israel. Paul's statement is an emphatic denial of such a charge. Others, however, prefer to see in these words an allusion to the consequences of the teaching of the Judaizers. They, by insisting upon obedience to Jewish law as a condition of salvation, did in fact nullify God's grace. The affirmation of verse 21b seems to support this interpretation: "for if righteousness is through the law, then Christ died for nought" (ASV). The idea is that righteousness comes either by the law or through the sacrificial death of Christ. It cannot be a combination of both. Indeed, Paul teaches in this statement that if a man could be justified by the law, then Christ died needlessly. The teaching of the Judaizers, then, makes the death of Christ a useless tragedy having no significance whatsoever.

FOR FURTHER STUDY

1. Read an article on Antioch (of Syria).
2. Read articles on "Grace" and "Justification" in a Bible dictionary.
3. Alexander Maclaren has a sermon on Galations 2:20 in his *Expositions of Holy Scripture*. Spurgeon has two sermons on the same text in his *Treasury of the New Testament*.

CHAPTER 5

The Truth of the Gospel:

The Doctrinal Argument

(Galatians 3:1 — 4:11)

In chapters 1 and 2 Paul has defended his apostolic authority. This he accomplished by an appeal to historical facts, showing that his apostleship was independent of that of the Jerusalem apostles (1:11-24), that it was fully recognized by them (2:1-10), and that on at least one occasion it was asserted in opposition to the leader of the Twelve (2:11-21). Having thus vindicated his authority, that is, his right to *proclaim* the Gospel, Paul is now ready to establish the *truth* of his Gospel, the essence of which is that justification comes through faith in Jesus Christ and that works of the law contribute nothing to it. This theme, which runs through chapters 3 and 4, is developed by means of doctrinal argument (3:1-4:11), personal entreaty (4:12-20), and allegorical interpretation (4:21-31).

Our concern in the present chapter is to trace the course of the doctrinal argument, the burden of which is to vindicate the Pauline Gospel against those who challenged its truth. In the development of his argument the apostle reminds the Galatians of their early Christian experience (3:1-5), cites the witness of Scripture (3:6-14), uses an analogy drawn from the customs of men (3:15-18), explains the role of the law (3:19-24), and describes the position of believers under the Gospel (3:25-4:11). The whole passage is a convincing refutation of the teaching of the Judaizers and a lucid exposition of the doctrine of justification by faith alone. The thought is profound, but is not particularly difficult to follow.

I. THE EXPERIENCE OF THE GALATIANS (3:1-5).

Here the apostle shows that the present attitude of the Galatians is a contradiction of their past spiritual experience. He reminds them that their entrance into the Christian life was effected not through the operation of law but by simple faith in Jesus Christ. This being so, they should not now attempt to perfect their experience by reversion to the law. The paragraph is made up almost entirely of questions, and the best way of explaining it is to take up each question in order.

1. First question: *O foolish Galatians, who did bewitch you, before whose eyes Jesus Christ was openly set forth crucified?* (verse 1, ASV). These words are an expression of surprise, perplexity, and indignation, somewhat reminiscent of the statement in 1:6. To Paul it was incredible that the Galatians were turning away from a Gospel of grace to a system of legal bondage. Their course of action made no sense in light of the character of Paul's preaching (verse 1) and in light of the marvelous things God had done for them in the wake of that preaching (verses 2-5).

"O foolish Galatians" is an exclamation of both condemnation and pity. The word rendered "foolish" suggests that the readers were acting unreasonably, that they were failing to use their mental powers. Moffatt uses the word "senseless." The NEB translates: "You stupid Galatians!" "The suggestion is that anyone with spiritual perception ought to be able to see the impossibility of legal efforts to save a man" (Guthrie, p. 95).

The present conduct of the Galatians was so irrational as to suggest that someone might have "bewitched" them. The word so translated suggests the art of a sorcerer in putting "an evil eye" on his victim. The TCNT reads, "Who has been fascinating you?" Knox renders it, "Who is it that has cast a spell on you." Paul, of course, did not believe that this was literally so. His use of the word is metaphorical and should be understood in the sense of "to confuse the mind."

Many interpreters think the words, "before whose eyes Jesus Christ was openly set forth," pick up the metaphor of the evil eye. In popular thinking this could take effect only if the eye of the victim met the sorcerer's gaze. The suggestion is that if the Galatians had only kept their gaze steadily fixed on the crucified Christ, they would have been immune to the malicious magic of the Judaizers.

"Was openly set forth," which translates a single Greek word, is an especially vivid expression. Its literal meaning, according to some, is "to write publicly," "to placard," or (if there were such a word) "to billboard." Lightfoot comments that it was used commonly for public notices and proclamations. According to this interpretation the apostle is saying that his preaching of Christ had the clarity of an advertisement on a billboard. Others, however, point to the fact that the root of the Greek word (*-grapho*) was used of a painter's art. (Compare our word "graphic" for what is vividly pictorial.) Thayer therefore suggests that the word here means "to depict (paint, portray) before the eyes."

The character in which Paul proclaimed Christ is indicated by the word "crucified." Placed at the end of the sentence for the sake of emphasis, it calls attention to the more dreadful features of Christ's death. In an earlier period the Romans had practiced crucifixion only in the case of slaves and the worst criminals. In New Testament times it probably was not confined to these classes but was extended to include others. It still retained, however, the idea of special disgrace. The tense of the Greek word emphasizes that the death of Jesus, though an event of the past, has results which continue into the present. Burton explains that it represents Christ "as one who was put to death on the cross, and thenceforth, the risen from the dead, the crucified one" (p. 145). "The Cross," writes Hunter, "is not a mere *past* fact, but a *present* reality, daily felt by men" (p. 26).

2. The second question makes direct appeal to the experience of the Galatians: *This only would I learn of you, Received ye the Spirit by the works of the law, or by the hearing of faith?* (verse 2). In effect, it means: How did you become Christians? The introductory words suggest that the apostle was willing to stake everything on this one question. He knew there could be only one answer, and that answer would settle the whole matter. Knox: "Let me be content with asking you one question."

The "Spirit" is of course the Holy Spirit, and the reception of the Spirit referred to is that which occurred when the Galatians embraced the Gospel. Some interpreters think the apostle's language points to the charismatic manifestations of the Spirit which may have accompanied the readers' entrance into the Christian life, but there is no express mention of such manifestations in the present verse.

The key phrases in Paul's question are "the works of the law" (i.e., works prescribed by law) and "the hearing of faith" (i.e., a hearing which leads to, and is therefore characterized by, faith). Moffatt interprets these to mean, respectively, "doing what the Law commands" and "believing the gospel message." Weymouth brings out the meaning clearly: "This one question I would ask you: Is it on the ground of obeying the Law that you received the Spirit, or is it because you heard and believed?" In short, the verse asks whether the Galatians received the Spirit *by works* or *by faith*. To ask the question was to answer it. Works obviously had nothing to do with it.

3. Third question: *Are ye so foolish?* [cf. verse 1 for the same word]

having begun in the Spirit, are ye now made perfect by the flesh?
(verse 3). Most of our Bibles print this verse as two questions. It is
obvious, however, that they are essentially one. There is a twofold
contrast in the question. "Beginning" is set over against "perfecting"
(completing), and "Spirit" is set over against "flesh."

"Having begun in the Spirit" reflects the truth that the Holy Spirit
is the element in which the Christian life has its beginning. "Are ye
now perfected in the flesh" (ASV) is an allusion to the fleshly ordinances and ceremonies of Judaism which the Galatians were being
urged to observe. The use of the word "perfected," which probably
was a term employed by the heretical teachers, shows that Paul's
readers did not think of themselves as abandoning Christianity entirely; they were, in their way of thinking, adding something (Jewish
law) to their Christian faith as a means of reaching perfection. Faith,
they probably said, is useful as a preliminary step, but law is needed
for the development of a mature religious life. Phillips' paraphrase expresses Paul's reaction: "Surely you can't be so idiotic as to think that
a man begins his spiritual life in the Spirit and then completes it by
reverting to outward observances."

4. Fourth question: *Have ye suffered so many things in vain? if it
be yet in vain* (verse 4). This is an appeal to the readers not to let
all that they have experienced in Christ be for nothing. The precise
meaning of the word "suffer" is debated. If the reference is to suffering
in the usual sense of that word (KJV, ASV), we are to conclude from
its occurrence here that the Galatians had endured great afflictions in
consequence of their becoming Christians. On this view Paul is asking
them whether they are prepared to look upon those afflictions as useless — as indeed they were if the Galatians should go off into Judaism.
Others, interpreting the Greek verb in the sense of "experience" (cf.
RSV), take the "many things" to refer to blessings. NEB: "Have all
your great experiences been in vain — if vain indeed they should be?"

In adding the words "if it be yet in vain" Paul implies that it is
hard for him to believe that the Galatians would abandon the Gospel
and embrace the teachings of the Judaizers. He expected better things
from them.

5. Fifth question: *He therefore that ministereth to you the Spirit,
and worketh miracles among you, doeth he it by the works of the law,
or by the hearing of faith?* (verse 5). This question, which recapitu-
lates the paragraph, picks up and develops more fully the thought
which was introduced in verse 2. That verse refers to the readers' reception of the Spirit in conversion and asks whether this was effected

by doing the works of the law or by hearing the Gospel with faith. This verse appeals to their present experience of the Spirit and asks on what grounds His gifts are imparted to them. That is to say, is it the result of "works of the law" or of "the hearing of faith."

"He . . . that ministereth to you the Spirit, and worketh miracles among you" is God. The word translated "ministereth" means "to bestow liberally," "to supply abundantly," "to lavish." The reference to the working of "miracles" is somewhat ambiguous. It could mean that God was working miracles "in" them (ASV margin; cf. 1 Cor. 12:28 and Matt. 14:2). Understood in this manner, the reference may be to the moral and spiritual transformation brought about in conversion; to bodily cures brought about in answer to prayer; or to spiritual gifts, such as prophecy, discerning of spirits, and so forth. Most interpreters, however, prefer the words "among you" (KJV, ASV, RSV, NEB). Understood in this manner the reference appears to be to outward deeds of a miraculous nature performed by the Galatians. Knox: "enables you to perform miracles."

The essential thought of the verse is not in question. It teaches that the gift of the Holy Spirit to the Galatians and His mighty working in and through them was dependent altogether on their faith in Christ.

II. THE TEACHING OF THE OLD TESTAMENT (3:6-14).

Having appealed to the Galatians' Christian experience, Paul now directs their attention to the witness of the Scriptures. His argument is that these also show that faith, not works, is the means of gaining a right standing before God. He begins with the testimony of the Old Testament concerning the faith of Abraham (verses 6-9); this is followed by a statement of its witness concerning the curse of the law (verses 10-14).

1. *The justification of Abraham* (verses 6-9). The argument here would carry special weight with the Judaizers, for it was customary for the rabbis to settle their controversies by precedents which they found in Abraham's life-story. He was venerated by all Jews as the founder of their race and was looked upon by them as a righteous man *par excellence*. Paul affirms that the patriarch was justified by faith and argues from this that only those of like faith participate with him in the divine blessing.

The phrase "Even as Abraham" shows that the experience of the Galatians (verses 1-5) and that of Abraham are essentially the same. The one serves to confirm the other.

How did this distinguished man gain his position of favor with

God? The answer is plain: *Abraham believed God, and it [his faith] was accounted to him for righteousness* (verse 6). The quotation, found also in Romans 4:3, is from the Septuagint version of Genesis 15:6. Paul's point is that faith, not works, brought Abraham's acceptance with God. Ridderbos points out that in the Genesis account Abraham's faith is seen as a "readiness to surrender unreservedly to the word of the Lord, regardless of how incredible it seemed" (Ridderbos, p. 118).

The word translated "accounted" ("reckoned," ASV) means to credit or charge something to one's account. The thought is that God accepted Abraham's faith as equivalent to righteousness. Cole comments: "Abraham entered into his particular blessing by realizing that he could do nothing for himself, confessing it to God, counting on God to do what he could not. . . . This attitude alone is 'right standing' with God, for any other attitude is stubborn pride and self-righteousness" (p. 91). The thought is developed more fully in Romans 4.

In verses 7-9 Paul shows that only those persons who have the faith of Abraham can properly be called the descendants of Abraham. The matter is succinctly stated in verse 7: *Know therefore that they that are of faith, the same are sons of Abraham* (ASV). The expression "they that are of faith" means believers — those whose fundamental life principle is faith, those who, like Abraham, believingly commit themselves to God. These only — the Greek word translated "the same" is emphatic — are the "sons of Abraham." The latter expression is used to designate Abraham's spiritual descendants. The Judaizers were teaching that to be sons of Abraham (and heirs of the promise made to him) they had to be circumcised, had, in fact, to become Jews. Paul teaches that circumcision has nothing to do with it, that spiritual kinship, not physical descent, is the determinative factor.

This thought is enlarged upon in verse 8. Since kinship with Abraham depends on faith, the promise given to him and his descendants can be shared by believing Gentiles. This, Paul affirms, is the express teaching of the Bible. *And the scripture, foreseeing that God would justify the Gentiles by faith, preached the gospel beforehand unto Abraham, saying, In thee shall all the nations be blessed* (verse 8). Paul personifies "scripture" and attributes to it personal activity (foreseeing and preaching).

What the Scripture *foresaw* was "that God would justify the Gentiles by faith" (ASV). The words "by faith" are, by their position in the sentence, emphatic. The tense of the verb "justify" is such as to express a general principle. The statement, therefore, is that justification by faith is God's rule of action in every age.

What the Scripture *preached* is stated at the close of verse 8: "In thee shall all the nations be blessed." Paul saw this divine promise as an advance announcement of the Gospel. It was, as Sieffert says, "an evangel before the evangel" (quoted by Hovey). The form of the quotation as given by Paul combines Genesis 12:3 and Genesis 18:18. The words "in thee" are not easy to explain. Probably they suggest that the nations are blessed in association with Abraham and the truth represented by him. (Compare verse 9, "blessed with . . . Abraham." He is at the head of a great company of believers.

The argument begun in verse 6 is summarized and concluded in verse 9: *So then they that are of faith are blessed with the faithful Abraham* (ASV). The emphasis is on the words "they that are of faith." That is to say, men of faith are the spiritual descendants of Abraham, not the doers of law. The Judaizers of course argued just the opposite, namely, that it was only those who were circumcised who could inherit the blessings promised to Abraham and his seed. "Blessed [in company] with . . . Abraham" expresses the same thought as "sons of Abraham" (verse 7). Paul describes the patriarch as "faithful" because as a believing man faith was the most distinguishing feature of his life.

2. *The curse of the law* (verses 10-14). In the preceding verses (6-9) Paul has used Scripture to prove that right standing before God comes through faith. Now, again appealing to Scripture, he shows that the law only can bring men into condemnation. The rabbis taught that the common people who had no interest in the law were under God's curse (cf. John 7:49). Here Paul teaches that all who seek acceptance with God on the grounds of obedience to law are under God's curse. *For as many as are of the works of the law* [i.e., all who rely on the law as a means of salvation] *are under a curse* (verse 10a, ASV), that is, separated from God. This is because it is not possible for anyone to fulfill the requirements of the law. Its testimony is, *Cursed is every one who continueth not in all things that are written in the book of the law, to do them* (verse 10b, ASV). The words are a free quotation from Deuteronomy 27:26, where they form the conclusion of the series of curses to be pronounced from Mt. Ebal. The minor changes made by Paul in citing the passage serve merely to bring out more distinctly its meaning. In his statement the emphasis rests on the words "continueth" and "all things," pointing up that the law demands perpetual and complete obedience.

Having shown in verse 10 that it is impossible to carry out the demands of the law and that the failure to do so puts men under a curse, the apostle now cites (verses 11, 12) two other Scriptures which show the inability of the law to justify. One of those Scriptures, Habakkuk 2:4, declares that faith, not works, is the source of life; the other, Leviticus 18:5, affirms that doing, not believing, is at the heart of the law. The two methods differ radically and are mutually exclusive. The manner in which Paul introduces these two Scriptures seems to imply that even if one were able to fulfill the law, continuing in all of its ordinances perfectly, it still could not save, for the spirit of the law is antagonistic to faith.

In its original setting the Habakkuk passage (*The righteous shall live by faith,* ASV) speaks of the righteous Israelite being preserved by his faithfulness (steadfast trust) in the midst of the ruin caused by the Babylonian invasion. Paul gives to the verse a deeper, more spiritual meaning than it had for Habakkuk, but he is not untrue to its germinal idea. In Paul's interpretation "the righteous" is equivalent to "the justified." Burton interprets the whole sentence to mean, "It is by faith that he who is approved of God is approved (and saved)" (p. 166).

The expression *and the law is not of faith* (verse 12a) means that faith is not the fundamental principle of the law, is not its starting point. The RSV reads, "but the law does not rest on faith." The working principle of the law is expressed in verse 12b: *The man that doeth them shall live in them.* Men are not commanded to believe the law but to do it. Obedience, not faith, is its central concept.

The previous verses (10-12) have depicted the desperate plight of those who seek justification by the works of law. Verses 13 and 14 assert that Christ, who sets men free from the curse of the law, is the one hope of salvation. The central thought is that He acted as our representative and substitute, taking upon Himself the penalty due to us for our sin (cf. 2 Cor. 5:21). At least three matters are to be observed: First, there is a statement of fact: *Christ redeemed us from the curse of the law* (verse 13a, ASV). The verb *"redeemed"* means "to deliver by the payment of a price," that is, "to buy out from." In everyday life it was used of purchasing a slave with a view to giving him his freedom or of ransoming prisoners of war. Ridderbos observes, however, that there is more here than simply the emancipation of a prisoner. "At issue here is satisfaction of violated justice. . . . Behind the imagery employed, there very probably lies the old practice . . . according to which ransom money could be paid for a forfeited life (cf. Exodus 21:30). According to this line of thought those who were under the curse were to be regarded not merely as prisoners but as persons appointed to die" (pp. 126, 127).

Second, Christ accomplished this deliverance by *being made a curse for us* (verse 13b). How He did this, we are not told. All we are told is that in some mysterious sense the curse of the law, which should have come upon us, fell on Him. The words *for it is written, Cursed is every one that hangeth on a tree* (verse 13c) are a kind of parenthesis. Taken from Deuteronomy 21:23, they show that the law itself proclaims the kind of death Christ died to be an example of the curse in action. In their original context these words do not refer to death on a cross, a practice unknown in ancient Israel. They refer rather to the practice of hanging the body of an executed criminal on a tree of shame. The point is that in His death, Christ's body also hung on a tree of shame, as though He were a condemned and executed criminal.

Third, the purpose of Christ's redemptive deed: *That upon the Gentiles might come the blessing of Abraham in Christ Jesus; that we might receive the promise of the Spirit through faith* (verse 14, asv). The two purpose clauses of this verse (introduced by "that") may be seen as coordinate. That is to say, they may express two separate and distinct purposes of Christ's work: (1) that the blessing of Abraham (i.e., justification by faith) might come on the Gentiles; and (2) that we (both Jews and Gentiles) might receive the promise of the Spirit (i.e., the promised Spirit) through faith. This interpretation is preferred by Burton and others. Lightfoot, on the other hand, thinks that the two clauses express a single purpose, that the second simply defines more precisely the meaning of the first. That is to say, "the blessing of Abraham" is interpreted to mean "the promise of the Spirit." There is much to be said for this view, for the Abrahamic promise surely finds its highest fulfillment in the activity of the Spirit in believing men. We prefer, however, the interpretation of Burton.

III. An analogy drawn from the customs of men (3:15-18).

Paul's opponents might have argued that since the law was given later than the promise, it was superior to, and might even supersede, it. Verses 15-18, which are Paul's answer, teach that God's promise to Abraham and his posterity was graciously bestowed and has permanent validity; its fulfillment can in no way be dependent upon the keeping of a law which came centuries after Abraham's time. To make obedience to law the condition of inheriting the blessing of the promise would be like cancelling or altering the will of another person. This simply is not done.

Paul introduces the paragraph by addressing his readers as "Brethren." This is an affectionate, friendly term, the tone of which contrasts sharply with that of the expressions used in 3:1, 3. *I speak after the manner of men* (verse 15a) suggests that Paul is about to draw an illustration from ordinary human life. "Brethren, I will take an illustration from everyday life." The illustration (or analogy) is this: *Though it be but a man's covenant, yet when it hath been confirmed, no one maketh it void, or addeth thereto* (verse 15b, ASV). The meaning is that even in ordinary human relationship a duly ratified contract or will (the word may mean either) is fixed and sacred. It cannot be set aside, nor can it be modified by adding new stipulations. If this is true even of a human will (or agreement), how much more true is it of a divine will (or agreement).

Verse 16, which comes in almost as a parenthesis, consists of an assertion and an explanation. The assertion brings out that God has indeed made a "will," it consists of "promises," and Abraham and his posterity are named as beneficiaries: *Now to Abraham and his seed were the promises made* (verse 16a). The passage which appears to have been uppermost in Paul's mind is Genesis 17:7-10, but the promise to Abraham is also recorded in Genesis 12:7; 13:15, 17; 22:18; and 24:7. This repetition of the promise from time to time probably accounts for the use of the plural "promises." The mention of Abraham's "seed" (offspring) shows that the benefits of the promise were not limited to Abraham, but extended to his posterity.

Paul's explanation of the promise is in verse 16b: *He saith not, And to seeds, as of many; but as of one, And to thy seed, which is Christ* (verse 16b). The main point is that the promise was given to a single person, not to many — to Abraham's "seed" (singular) not to his "seeds" (plural). The word for seed, to be sure, is used in the Genesis passage in a collective sense; we may be confident that Paul was fully aware of this. He is insisting, however, that the singular form is especially appropriate in view of the fact that the fulfillment of the promise is realized at its deepest level only in Christ. The sense of this whole verse is clearly expressed in the TCNT: "Now it was to Abraham that the promises were made, 'and to his offspring.' It was not said 'to his offspring,' as if many persons were meant, but the words were 'to thy offspring,' showing that one person was meant — and that was Christ."

Verse 17 picks up the thought of the fifteenth verse. The words

And this I say are Paul's way of saying, "This is what I mean." TCNT:
"My point is this." Having mentioned that human wills (or agree-
ments) once ratified cannot be set aside or altered, the apostle now
affirms that the same principle holds true. of the will or agreement
made by God with Abraham. It was *confirmed beforehand by God,*
[and] *the law, which came four hundred and thirty years after,* [can-
not] *disannul* (unmake) [it], so as to make the [Abrahamic] *promise
of none effect* (i.e., render it inoperative, cancel it). Whatever else
the law may have been intended to do, it surely was not meant to set
aside or to alter the terms of the promise of justification through faith.

Questions have been raised concerning the chronology mentioned
in this verse. The period of "four hundred and thirty years" from
Abraham to the Exodus appears to be in conflict with Exodus 12:40,
which states that the sojourn of the Israelites *in Egypt* was 430 years.
(Compare Acts 7:6, where Stephen, though using 400 as a round
number, also suggests that this entire period was spent in Egypt.)
Two things may be said in reference to this difficulty. First, Paul appears to have followed the reading of the Septuagint version of Exodus
12:40, which makes "four hundred and thirty years" the period of
time spent "in the land of Egypt *and in the land of Canaan.*" This
version was the one familiar to his readers and was sufficiently ac-
curate for his immediate purposes. A second thing to keep in mind is
that Paul's argument is not in the least weakened whether we follow
the reading of the Septuagint or of the Hebrew text. His point is
that the law was given long after the promise and could not destroy or
change it. Whatever the length of the time period, the argument is
the same.

Verse 18a teaches that there can be no compromise between law
and promise: *For if the inheritance be of the law, it is no more of
promise.* Bruce's paraphrase brings out the sense: "Now, if the inheritance of Abraham is based on the law, it can no longer be regarded as resting on God's promise." Law and promise are so funda-
mentally different that they can in no way be combined.

In the context of Abraham's life the "inheritance" was the possession
of the promised land (cf. Gen. 12:7; 13:15, 17; 17:8; 24:7), but Paul
sees in the word a deeper reference to all the spiritual blessings obtained through faith in Christ.

Verse 18b teaches that true heirship comes by divine gift, not by
human merit. *God gave it [the inheritance] to Abraham by promise.*
The Greek word for "gave," which is built on the root word for grace,
was employed in legal documents as a technical term for making a

grant, deeding something by will. Its use here calls attention to the freeness of the divine bestowal. The tense (perfect) emphasises the permanence of the gift.

IV. THE ROLE OF THE LAW (3:19-24).

Paul thinks of two objections that might be raised with reference to his teaching concerning the promise and the inability of the law to affect that promise. Both objections take the form of questions: *What then is the law?* (verse 19a, ASV) and *Is the law then against the promises of God?* (verse 21a). In answering these questions the apostle expounds the true role of the law.

1. *The law as a temporary and inferior system* (verses 19, 20). The first question has to do with the significance of the law in the scheme of redemption. The RSV puts it, "Why then the law?" That is, if God never intended that men should be justified by it, what end does it serve? Why was it given? What is the reason for its existence? Paul's answer is given in verse 19b: *It was added because of transgressions, till the seed should come to whom the promise hath been made; and it was ordained through angels by the hand of a mediator* (ASV). Three truths, each pointing up the inferiority of the law, are embedded in this statement: First, the law was not a part of the original covenant made with Abraham; it "was added" at a later time. Bruce: "It was an extra dispensation." It was introduced "because of transgressions" (lit., "for the sake of transgressions"). These words are interpreted variously. Some, for example, take the preposition to have *retrospective* force and interpret the whole phrase to mean that the law was given to restrain transgressions, to check their growing number. Others, interpreting the preposition as having *prospective* force, understand the phrase to mean that the law was given in order to expose sin, that is, to give it the character of transgression. In so doing the law intensifies man's consciousness of guilt and arouses the desire for redemption.

Second, the legal system was a temporary arrangement — valid only "till the seed should come," etc. To say the least, these words suggest that the importance of the law was intended to diminish after Christ's coming. Luther observed that Paul's statement is true both literally and spiritually — literally, in the sense that the era of law lasted only until Christ came; spiritually, in the sense that in the individual conscience the law does not reign after Christ has entered.

Third, the law "was ordained through angels by the hand of a mediator." Nothing is said in the Book of Exodus of the place of angels in the giving of the law, but their presence is referred to in Deuteronomy 33:2 (cf. Acts 7:53 and Heb. 2:2). We have no way of knowing exactly what their service was. The point is that their very presence as well as that of the "mediator" (Moses) served to diminish rather than to increase the importance of the legal system. The dignity and sacredness of the promise, which was given directly by God to Abraham, far surpasses that of the law.

Verse 20 continues this line of thought: *Now a mediator ["intermediary," RSV] is not a mediator of one, but God is one* (ASV). Someone has estimated that more than three hundred interpretations have been given of this verse, but most present-day commentaries are in essential agreement as to its meaning. The idea is that the very presence of a mediator (Moses) at the giving of the law implies two other parties (God and the people). Two conclusions may be drawn from this: First, the giving of the law was not a direct communication of God to those who were to receive its benefits. This is a mark of the law's inferiority to the promise, which was communicated directly to Abraham without an intermediary. Second, the law, being a kind of contract between two parties (God and the people), was dependent upon both for its effectiveness.

"But God is one" means that the promise, unlike the law, was made without an intermediary. Bruce paraphrases: "but when God made His promise He acted on His own sovereign account." The promise therefore is absolute and unconditional, dependent for its fulfillment solely upon God, by whom alone it was made.

2. *The law as preparatory* (verses 21-24). Paul anticipates a second objection to his teaching in the question, *Is the law then against the promises of God?* (verse 21a). That is to say, if the law is what Paul has just declared it to be, a temporary and inferior arrangement, does it by its very nature contradict the promises? Are we to conclude that there is antagonism between these two expressions of the divine will? The very thought is abhorrent to Paul, and he dismisses it immediately with "God forbid." The NEB: "No, never!"

It was obvious to Paul, however, that the law was not meant, nor was it able, to give life. If a law had been given which could impart life, then legalism would have been the way of gaining acceptance with God (verse 21). But as it is, *the scripture shut up all things under [i.e., in the prison-house of] sin [in order], that the promise by [based on] faith in Jesus Christ might be given to them that believe* (verse 22, ASV). "The scripture" refers to the Old Testament, especially the law. "Shut up" ("concluded," KJV) means consigned,

locked up conclusively with no power of escape. "All things" is a
more emphatic way of referring to "all men," the whole race. "Under
sin" means under the condemnation of sin.

The purpose of the shutting up is expressed in the words "that the
promise by faith in Jesus Christ might be given to them that believe"
(verse 22b, ASV). The meaning is, that it might be made clear that
there is but one way open to men of gaining acceptance with God —
the way of faith in Jesus Christ. "The promise," which is to be understood in the sense of "the fulfillment of the promise" is practically
equivalent to justification, acceptance with God. The double reference
to faith ("by faith" and "them that believe") brings out its special
importance.

The law and the promise therefore are not contradictory; they are
complementary. Both have a part in the plan of God, and in this plan
the law is subservient to the promise. It has not the power to impart
life, but it does have a function to fulfill. By making men aware of
their sin, their guilt, and their impotence to achieve salvation, the law
creates in them a longing for the deliverance that only Christ can
bring.

Verses 23 and 24, which give further development of the preparatory function of the law, represent the law as a jailor (verse 23) and
as a "pedagogue" or custodian (verse 24). Both figures point up that
the law was a necessary discipline preparing us for sonship in Christ.

First, the law as a jailor: *Before faith came,* writes Paul, *we were
kept in ward under the law, shut up unto the faith that should
afterwards be revealed* (verse 23, ASV). "Before faith came" means
before the Gospel era, that is, before the coming of the Messiah. It is
not that faith was a new principle. Faith always has been the means
by which God saves men, as Paul has made abundantly clear in the
references to Abraham. But faith in its distinctive character as trust
in Jesus Christ did in a sense come with the opening of the Messianic
era.

The verb translated "we were kept in ward" may denote either restrictive or protective guarding. Elsewhere in the New Testament (2
Cor. 11:32; Phil. 4:7; 1 Pet. 1:5) it has the latter sense. Here, however, it connotes restrictive guarding. In military circles it was used
of shutting off avenues of escape, as in a siege. The pronoun "we"
probably refers to Paul and his fellow Jews. The Galatians had, of
course, never lived under the Mosaic law. Ridderbos thinks, however,
that Paul was including his Gentile readers, for though they were
"outside the pale of the revelation to Israel," they "were co-subject to

the law with the Jews, and were not without knowledge of it (Rom. 2:14-16)" (p. 145).

"Shut up unto the faith which should afterwards be revealed" shows that those under the law were in a sense guarded and kept with a view to their eventually passing over into faith. "The bondage under the law urged and forced man towards the faith" (Ridderbos, pp. 144, 145). This "faith" is primarily subjective faith (trust) in Jesus Christ, but there is at least a tinge of the objective sense of the word, that is, a system of doctrine which has faith as its distinguishing feature.

Second, the law as a custodian: *Wherefore the law was [has proved itself to be] our schoolmaster to bring us unto Christ, that we might be justified by faith* (verse 24). "Schoolmaster" translates the word of which the word "pedagogue" is a transliteration. The RSV renders it "custodian"; Phillips, "a strict governess." The Greek word, which literally means "child-guide," was not used of a teacher but of an attendant of minor boys. Ordinarily the pedagogue was a trusted slave who had responsibility for the moral training and general protection of a boy between the ages of six and sixteen. The pedagogue watched over the child's behavior and attended him when he was away from home. Often the pedagogues treated their charges with harshness and severity. By calling the law "our pedagogue," Paul emphasizes two things: (1) the disciplinary (not the educative) character of the law and (2) the inferior condition of those under the law. The latter are like children who have not yet arrived at the freedom of a mature person.

"Unto Christ" suggests either the aim of the custodial work of the law or its temporal limits. The KJV rendering "to bring us unto Christ," suggests the former; RSV and NEB interpret in the latter sense, "until Christ came." The Greek expression, which literally means "with a view to Christ," leaves room for either of these interpretations. Bruce paraphrases it, "keeping us safe for Christ." Christ having come, the law hands us over to Him "that we might be justified by faith" (verse 24c).

Weymouth's rendering seems to express the meaning of the verse: "So that the law has proved a tutor to discipline us for Christ, that through faith we may be justified."

V. THE STATUS OF BELIEVERS UNDER THE GOSPEL (3:25-4:11).

The immediately preceding verses have delineated life under the law, "before faith came" (verse 23). The present passage characterizes life under the Gospel, "now that faith is come" (verse 25, ASV). The state of those under the law was one of immaturity and bondage. The state of those who are in Christ is that of "sons" and "heirs."

One should keep in mind that Paul's opponents, who were doing all in their power to get the Galatian Christians to submit to the regulations of the law, represented life under the law as the ultimate ideal. They argued that something was missing in the life of a believer until he submitted to the binding authority of the law. In opposition to this Paul has shown that life under the law was never meant to be the ideal and that it is in every way inferior to life in Christ. Jews under the law, he has argued, were like children under age; the law at best had served only as a guide to prepare them for the acceptance of the Messiah. In this paragraph he shows that faith brings men into the dignity of full grown sons (with the privilege of free access to the Father) and to the full possession of their rightful heritage. A return to law, then, could in no way be looked upon as an advance in the Christian life. It was a turning back from a state of spiritual maturity and freedom to a condition of spiritual immaturity and bondage.

The entire paragraph may be divided into three parts: In the first (3:25-29) the believer's status is affirmed; in the second (4:1-7) essentially the same ground is covered, but a fuller explanation is given; in the third (4:8-11) the doctrinal argument is concluded by a brief discussion of the personal aspects of the Galatian controversy.

1. *A statement of the believer's position* (verses 25-29). The essence of these verses may be summed up as follows: First, believers are all full-grown sons of God (verses 25-27). *But now that faith [in Jesus Christ] is come, we are no longer under a tutor* (verse 25, ASV). The thought is that with the coming of the Messianic era the religious condition of believers has changed. *For ye are all sons of God, through faith, in Christ Jesus* (verse 26, ASV). Paul changes from "we" (verse 25) to "ye" in order to apply his argument more forcefully to his readers. The Greek word for "all" stands first in the sentence and is therefore emphatic. The Judaizers claimed that those who submitted to the rites of the law were in a superior position to non-circumcised Gentile believers. In marked contrast to this, Paul affirms that all of his readers, whether of Jewish or of Gentile background, have the dignity and privileges of full-grown sons of God.

"In Christ Jesus" may be construed either with "sons of God" or with "through faith." The KJV takes it in the latter sense: "For ye are all children of God by faith in Christ Jesus." The NEB expresses the former idea: "For through faith you are all sons of God in union with Christ Jesus" (cf. ASV, RSV). Thus two ideas are stressed: (1) Sonship to God is a state of intimate union with Christ and (2) it is realized by means of faith.

Verse 27 confirms the assertion that all believers are sons of God. *For as many of you as were baptized into Christ did put on Christ* (verse 27, ASV; cf. Rom. 6:3-11). Baptism, of course, is the means by which believers openly confess their relation to Christ. Baptized "into Christ" might at first appear to suggest that baptism actually effects this relation. This interpretation, however, runs counter to the whole tenor of Scripture. A better rendering might be "baptized in reference to Christ." In 1 Corinthians 10:2 the same formula is used of the Israelites being baptized "into [in reference to] Moses."

"Did put on Christ" ("have all put on Christ as a garment," NEB) emphasizes the closeness of the believer's relation to Christ. Just as a garment envelops the person who wears it, so Christ envelops the Christian. In addition, there is a suggestion of the believer's likeness to Christ. Moffatt brings out this idea: "for all of you who had your-selves baptized into Christ have taken on the character of Christ" (Compare Phillips: "have put on the family likeness of Christ.") Some scholars think the figure is taken from such Old Testament passages as Job 8:22 ("clothed with shame"), Job 29:14 ("I put on righteous-ness, and it clothed me"), Psalm 35:26 ("clothed with shame and dis-honour"), and Judges 6:34 ("the spirit of the LORD took possession of Gideon," NEB). Others think Paul's words are an allusion to the ceremony at which a Roman youth, passing from boyhood to man-hood, laid aside the clothing (*toga praetexta*) which marked him as a child and was invested with the clothing (*toga virilis*) which marked him as a mature man.

Second, believers are all one in Christ: *There is neither Jew nor Greek, there is neither bond nor free, there is neither male or female: for ye are all one in Christ Jesus* (verse 28). The NEB is better: "There is no such thing as Jew and Greek, slave and freeman, male and female; for you are all one person in Christ Jesus." It is not that distinctions of race, social standing, and sexuality are totally obliterated among Christians. But as barriers to fellowship they have no place in the Christian community. Those who are in Christ, in spite of his-torical and physical distinctions, form one great spiritual fellowship; they are all "one person in Christ Jesus" (NEB). Or, as Burton puts it, they "merge into one personality" (p. 208). The thought is similar to that which is found in Romans 12:4, 5; 1 Corinthians 10:17; 12:12, 13; and Colossians 3:15.

Third, believers are all heirs: *And if ye be Christ's, then are ye*

Abraham's seed, and heirs according to the promise (verse 29). The
"if" clause assumes the reality of the condition. The thought, is "And
since you belong to Christ" (TCNT). The first pronoun is emphatic:
"you Galatians, Gentiles though you are, are Christ's people." Cole
thinks the Greek behind these last words might almost be paraphrased,
"you are part of Christ's body" (p. 111). It follows, then, that Gentile
believers, no less than Jewish believers, are the offspring of Abraham
(cf. 3:6-9, 16). And so, they are heirs (sharers in the inheritance),
not by law and physical descent, but "according to [by] promise"
(ASV). These last words may be taken to mean "in fulfillment of the
promise."

Williams sums up Paul's argument in a single sentence: "You want
to be heirs of all that true relationship to Abraham brings — you have
obtained it in Christ" (p. 84).

2. *A further explanation of the believer's position* (4:1-7). These
verses restate in graphic, summary fashion the essential difference between Judaism and Christianity. The former, described in verses 1-3,
is a bondage and the position of its devotees is like that of children
who are kept under guardians and stewards. The latter, discussed in
verses 4-6, is a higher, more mature state; its adherents are lifted to
the dignity of sons and heirs of God and have their adoption as sons
sealed by the presence of the Holy Spirit in their hearts.

a. *Life under Judaism* (verses 1-3). To illustrate this Paul uses a
figure drawn from the customs of the day. *But I say that so long as
the heir is a child, he differeth nothing from a bondservant though he
is lord of all; but is under guardians and stewards until the day appointed of the father* (verses 1, 2, ASV). The situation described is not
that of a *dead* father, whose position the son assumes at the proper
age. It is rather the case of a *living* father who decides to give his son
a settlement when the latter attains to a certain age. The age itself —
whether eighteen, twenty-one, etc. — is unimportant; the point is that
it is fixed by the father and until the son reaches it he does not enter
upon his inheritance.

"But I say" (4:1a) is a transitional phrase showing that the apostle
is about to explain something which has been said in the preceding
verses. The RSV: "I mean that. . . ." The point of connection is the
word "heirs,"(3:29) which is here picked up and given fuller treatment. The Greek word for "child" probably is used in the general
sense of one who is not yet an adult. Such a person may be the heir
of all that his father owns, but so long as he is a child he "differeth
nothing from a bond servant" (4:1b). The NEB: "he is no better off

than a slave." The reference is to the lack of freedom of action. Knox's rendering expresses it: "one who comes into property while he is still a child has no more liberty than one of the servants, though all the estate is his."

Verse 2 explains this. The minor child, though potentially owner of all that has been bequeathed to him, "is under guardians and stewards until the day appointed of the father." Ordinarily a rigid distinction was not made between the Greek words for "guardians" and "stewards," but here, where both terms are used together, a distinction probably is intended. The "guardian" — the word is a general expression denoting "one to whose care something is committed" — was charged with the responsibility of looking after the *person* of an underaged child. The "steward" was responsible for the *property* of the child. "The day appointed of the father" is the time set by the father for the son to enter upon his destined inheritance.

Verse 3 makes the application: *So we also, when we were children, were held in bondage under the rudiments of the world* (ASV). That is to say, the manner in which human fathers arrange for and manage the affairs of their minor children is illustrative of the manner in which the heavenly Father has provided for His people. It is debated whether the "we" refers to all Christians or only to Jewish Christians. Perhaps the primary reference is to Jewish believers, but in a general sense Gentile believers may also be included.

Prior to their coming to Christ, both Jews and Gentiles "were held in bondage under the rudiments of the world." The word for "rudiments," which originally denoted things arranged in a row, has at least three meanings: (1) the letters of the alphabet, (2) the elements (ABC's) of a discipline or religion (cf. Heb. 5:12), and (3) the elements (substance) of the physical universe (cf. 2 Pet. 3:10-12). Some scholars understand the use of the word in the present passage in the second sense. This interpretation is reflected in the rendering of the TCNT: "the puerile teaching of this world." Williams, who also subscribes to this view, explains the phrase to mean "the A, B, C, of outward things, elementary beggarly rules connected with the external and the visible." He cites as examples, "the observance of sabbaths, new moons, etc. (verse 10), as ordered in the Law, written or oral, or the many ceremonies of the heathen" (p. 88).

Most recent interpreters understand the reference to be to the heavenly bodies and the spirit powers associated with them. This approach is reflected in the NEB: "the elemental spirits of the universe." The problem with this interpretation is that bondage to the heavenly bodies (or elemental powers) does not appear to have been characteristic of Judaism. Hunter, however, feels that Jews no less than Gentiles believed their destinies were "at the mercy of sinister heavenly powers." "We know," he writes, "that they linked the Law with angelic beings (3:19). Furthermore, the Jewish festivals, about whose observance the Galatians were so fussy (4:10), were fixed by the movements of the heavenly bodies. Thus, Paul can lump both the Law ritual of the Jews and the idolatry of the Gentiles together, calling them alike slavery to these elemental powers" (p. 32).

If the Greek word is interpreted in the sense of "rudiments" (i.e., elementary instruction), then "of the world" marks that instruction as material and external. If the word is understood as referring to the heavenly bodies or elemental spirits, "world" must be interpreted in the sense of "universe."

b. *The change brought by Christ* (verses 4-7). The coming of Christ into the world changed everything. This is stated in verses 4 and 5: *but when the fulness of the time came, God sent forth his Son, born of a woman, born under the law, that he might redeem them that were under the law, that we might receive the adoption of sons* (ASV). The central affirmation of these verses, "God sent forth his Son" (verse 4), is rich with meaning. At least three profound truths are involved in it: (1) the Son's pre-existence, (2) His investment with authority — the verb means "to send on a mission," and (3) His essential deity.

The context describes and defines this momentous event. First, it was in "the fulness of time" (verse 4a). The imagery suggests that the pre-Christian era was like "an unfilled measure which each year filled, as it were drop by drop, until the fulness of it came" (Williams, p. 88). There is an obvious allusion to verse 2 — "the time appointed by the father." The meaning is that the coming of Christ into the world was by divine appointment, God in His own wisdom determining when the time was right.

Second, the Son's mission was effected under specific historical conditions. He was "born of woman, born under the law" (verse 4b, RSV). The first phrase, which suggests the thought of weakness and condescension, emphasizes Christ's real humanity. There seems to be no special stress on the idea of His being virgin born, but the statement is in no way antithetical to the doctrine of the virgin birth. "Born under the law" means that Jesus was a Jew, subject to the restrictions, requirements, and demands of the law. Hunter suggests that this was "providentially arranged, so that the Son might learn sympathy with sinners and those in bondage" (pp. 32, 33).

Third, the purpose of Christ's coming is defined in terms of redemption and adoption. The former idea is stated in verse 5a: "that he might redeem them that were under the law" (ASV). The thought here is that Christ came to buy men out of bondage to the law and to deliver them from its sentence of condemnation. From 3:13, where the same verb is used, we learn that Christ did this by taking upon Himself the curse of the law. Adoption as sons, which is the ultimate purpose of Christ's coming, is stated in verse 5b: "that we [all of us — Jews and Gentiles] might receive the adoption of sons" (ASV). These words are an allusion to a Graeco-Roman legal device which permitted a wealthy man having no children to take into his family a slave youth and make him a son and heir. The use of the expression here draws attention to the fact that whereas Christ is Son by nature (verse 4), we are sons by grace.

The proof that believers are sons is given in verse 6: *And because ye are sons, God sent forth the Spirit of his Son into our hearts, crying Abba, Father* (ASV). It is not clear whether the first word in the Greek of verse 6 should be translated "because," indicating a reason for giving the Spirit (cf. KJV, ASV), or "as proof that," indicating that the gift of the Spirit is proof of sonship (cf. NEB). Both interpretations express very precious truth, but since the apostle's purpose was to convince his readers that they were sons of God, we prefer the latter. The meaning then is that the presence of the Spirit in the heart is a witness to the reality of the believer's sonship to God (cf. Rom. 8:14-16; Gal. 3:2).

The Greek word for "hath sent forth" is identical with that used in verse 4 of God's sending His Son into the world. "Crying" translates a word which denotes "earnest and importunate prayer" (Lightfoot, p. 169). "Abba," an Aramaic word having something of the familiar connotation of the English word "daddy," was used by Jewish children in addressing their earthly fathers and by Jesus in addressing His heavenly Father (Mark 14:36). The use of the two words "Abba, Father" may be intended to emphasize the intensity and the joy with which the believer approaches God in prayer. Since "Father" is preceded in Greek by the article, the whole phrase may be rendered "Abba, our Father."

Verse 7 sums up the paragraph. Believers are no longer slaves, but sons, and since they are sons they are heirs "through God" (ASV). Goodspeed's translation puts it: *So you are no longer a slave, but a son; and if a son, then an heir, made so by God.* The use of the second person singular pronoun individualizes the statement.

Each of the apostle's readers is thus reminded of his exalted privilege in the Gospel and of his debt of gratitude to God.

3. *The personal aspects of the Galatial controversy* (verses 8-11). By carefully reasoned arguments Paul has established that it is faith in Christ, not obedience to law, that makes men sons and heirs of God. With the exception of the opening paragraph (3:1-5) the discussion has for the most part concerned general principles. Now, as the apostle rounds out his argument, he returns to the more personal aspects of the controversy in which he is engaged. To state it otherwise, the present paragraph (verses 8-11) takes the results of the preceding argument and applies them to the case of the readers.

The drift of the passage may be summarized as follows: Before their conversion, the Galatians had lived as pagans. When they became Christians they were released from bondage to idol worship and were brought into the knowledge of the true God. Now they are being enticed to embrace a system which would again bring them into bondage — the bondage of Jewish law. Paul finds it incredible that anyone who has tasted the freedom of Christ should even think of putting himself under the servitude of the law. He seems to say again, "O foolish Galatians, who has bewitched you? After so great a change, how can you go back!"

In verses 8, 9a, which contrast what readers once were with what they now are, the key expressions are "at that time" (verse 8, ASV) and "but now" (verse 9, ASV; cf. Eph. 2:11-13). Their pre-Christian state was one of ignorance of God and enslavement to deities which were not really such. As Christians they "have come to know God, or rather to be known by God" (ASV). To "know" God is to be in vital fellowship with Him; to be "known by" God is to have Him acknowledge us as His own.

The remainder of the passage (verses 9b-11) is an expression of Paul's distress at the thought that the Galatians would turn back to a state of fear and bondage. *How turn ye back again to the weak and beggarly rudiments, whereunto ye desire to be in bondage over again?* (verse 9b, ASV). "Turn," which translates a present tense verb, suggests that the Galatians were already in process of turning back "to the weak and beggarly rudiments." This latter expression is Paul's description of the legalistic system being propagated by the Judaizers. The word for "rudiments" was used in verse 3 and is discussed above. The two adjectives, "weak" and "beggarly," point up the ineffectualness and poverty of Judaism as contrasted with the power and richness of the Gospel. "Over again" suggests that in Paul's mind the legalism of the Judaizers and the paganism of the Gentiles were in principle the same. Luther's comment is apropos: "Doth Paul take it to be all one thing, to fall from the promise to the law, from faith to works, and to do service unto gods which by nature are no gods? I answer: whosoever is fallen from the article of Justification, is ignorant of God, and an idolator. . . . The reason is, because God will or can be known no otherwise than by Christ. . . . There is no mean between man's working and the knowledge of Christ. If this knowledge be darkened or defaced, it is all one whether thou be a Monk, a Turk, a Jew, etc."

Verse 10 reveals that Paul's readers already had begun to keep some of the special times of the Jewish religious calendar. The word translated "observe" is intensive, suggesting a rigid observance. The TCNT translates it, "You are scrupulous in observing." In this context it means to observe or keep religiously. "Days" has reference to the weekly sabbaths (cf. Rom. 14:5; Col. 3:16). "Months" refers to the celebration of the appearance of the new moon at the first of each month (cf. Num. 10:10; 28:11; 1 Chron. 23:31; Psa. 81:3; Isa. 1:13; Hosea 2:11). "Seasons" probably refers to celebrations not limited to a single day, such as the feasts of Passover, Pentecost, and Tabernacles. The reference to "years" is understood by some to mean the seventh (sabbatic) year and the fiftieth (Jubilee) year. Others, however, think the reference is to the celebration of the beginning of the year in the month Tishri.

Perhaps we should not attempt to define the "days," "months," "seasons," and "years" of the text too precisely. The four terms may be listed simply as including all kinds of celebrations which were observed by the Jews. Paul's intent in mentioning them is to point up to the Galatians that their religion "has degenerated into an external formalism" (Stott, p. 108).

In view of the Galatians' attraction to Jewish legalism, the apostle expresses fear that the labor bestowed on them has been in vain, that is "without effect," "to no purpose" (verse 11; cf. 3:4). "These words," comments Luther, "breathe the tears of Paul." The whole statement shows that in the apostle's thinking a return to legalism was tantamount to a renunciation of Christ and a rejection of the Gospel.

FOR FURTHER STUDY

1. Read Genesis 12 and 15.
2. Read articles on "Faith," "Works," "Law," "Promise," "Abra-

ham," "Covenant," "Adoption," "Heirs," "Rudiments," and "Elemental Spirits" in a Bible dictionary.

3. Maclaren has sermons on Galatians 3:3, 4, 22; and 4:4 and 5.

4. Spurgeon has six sermons on the Scriptures treated in this chapter. See especially "Life by Faith" (Gal. 3:11), "Christ Made a Curse for Us" (Gal. 3:13), "The Great Jail, and How to Get Out of It" (Gal. 3:22), and "The Stern Pedagogue" (Gal. 3:24, 25).

CHAPTER 6

The Truth of Paul's Gospel:

The Personal Appeal

(Galatians 4:12-20)

The tone of the letter to this point has been intensely argumentative. The errors of the Judaizing system have been exposed and the principle of faith has been expounded and established. But since Paul is still unsure of his readers, he turns now to entreaty, and in a spirit of loving persuasion begs the Galatians to take his attitude toward the law. He reminds them of the devotion which they had manifested toward him at an earlier time and wonders what has happened to change that. He acknowledges that the Judaizers are courting the Galatians, but warns that their intentions are not honorable. The apostle closes the paragraph with the expression of a fervent wish that he could be present with them so that they might hear the affectionate tone of his voice. Perhaps this would help where all else has failed. If not, he is at a loss to know what to do. Throughout the paragraph, which is intensely personal, Paul pleads for the love and loyalty of his readers.

I. THE APPEAL (4:12a).

The appeal itself is found in verse 12a: *I beseech you, brethren, become as I am [in my freedom from the law], for I also am become as ye are* (ASV). The NEB: "Put yourselves in my place, my brothers, I beg you, for I have put myself in yours." What Paul means is that he wishes the Galatians to experience the same full freedom from the law that he has experienced. Once he had been zealous for the law (cf. 1:14) and had possessed all its advantages; in becoming a Christian, however, he had laid aside all these supposed advantages (cf. Phil. 3:7) and thereafter, in relation to the law, had lived in Gentile fashion (cf. 2:14). (Elsewhere [1 Cor. 9:21] he tells us that this disregard of Jewish conventions was to the end that he might more effectively witness to the Gentiles.) Now the Galatians are tempted to embrace the legal system which Paul had renounced, thinking that they will thereby gain for themselves greater acceptance with God. Paul knows that this reasoning is erroneous. He urges them therefore to take their place beside him, to be free as he is free.

The word "brethren" gives a tone of affection to the appeal and serves to remind the Galatians that Paul identifies himself with them. "Beseech," a word sometimes used of prayer to God, suggests the intensity of Paul's feeling.

II. THE GROUNDS OF THE APPEAL (4:12b-20).

The apostle's appeal is based upon two things: (1) their affection for Paul (verses 12b-16) and (2) his affection for them (verses 17-20).

1. *The Galatians' affection for Paul* (verses 12b-16). The connection of "Ye did me no wrong" (verse 12b, ASV) is not easy to determine. The KJV construes the words with what precedes, ASV and RSV with what follows. Their precise force is even more difficult to apprehend. Some scholars put stress on the significance of the tense (aorist) of the verb and understood Paul to be saying: "You did not *in the past* wrong me, but *now* you do." Burton, speaking more specifically, says Paul is replying to an assertion of the Galatians that they had done him no wrong, that it was their right to accept his message or to reject it. Paul concedes that they did him no wrong in their earlier association with him, but intimates (verse 16) that they are now wronging him in counting him their enemy. Perhaps we should simply understand Paul to mean, "My past experience with you encourages me to appeal to you in this manner, for I have never received anything but kindness from you."

An example of their generous and affectionate treatment of the apostle is cited in verses 13 and 14: *Ye know how through infirmity of the flesh I preached the gospel unto you at the first. And my temptation which was in my flesh ye despised not, nor rejected; but received me as an angel of God, even as Christ Jesus.*

"At the first" translates a Greek expression which may, under certain conditions, mean "formerly" (as in John 6:62; 1 Tim. 1:13, et al.), but probably here it is to be given its more literal sense, "the former time" (cf. ASV, "the first time"). This reading of the passage implies that the apostle had, before writing this letter, preached among the Galatians on two different occasions. If Galatians was written to the people of South Galatia, the first visit was on the first missionary journey (Acts 13:14 — 14:23) and the second was on the second journey (Acts 16:1-5). If the epistle was intended for the people of

North Galatia, the first visit (according to the proponents of the North
Galatian theory) was that of the second missionary journey (Acts
16:6) and the second was that of the third journey (Acts 18:23).

The occasion of the apostle's first preaching to the Galatians was
"an infirmity of the flesh" ("bodily ailment," RSV). Burton explains
that these words "can refer" only to some physical ailment hard to
bear, and calculated to keep [Paul] humble and, in some measure, to
repel those to whom he preached" (p. 239). What this affliction was
is much debated. Epilepsy, eye trouble, malaria — these are some of
the theories which have been propounded. But whatever the illness
was, Paul says it was the occasion for his preaching to the Galatians.
The idea may be that the illness detained him in the region of Galatia
longer than he had originally planned to stay, or it could be that it
was his illness that brought him to Galatia, contrary to previous plans.

The repulsive nature of the disease, whatever it was, is suggested
by the language of verse 14a: "and that which was a temptation
[test, trial] to you in my flesh ye despised not, nor rejected" (ASV).
The last two verbs are very strong; the former suggests scorn and
contempt, the latter literally means "to spit out." Both imply that
Paul's infirmity was of such a nature as to arouse feelings of repug-
nance in those who saw him. He seems to have feared that the Galatians would reject both him and his message, but they did not; instead,
they welcomed him as if he had been an angel of God — or even
Christ Jesus Himself (verse 14b).

The question of verse 15a grows out of what has just been said
about the enthusiastic reception given by the Galatians to Paul and
his message. *Where then is that gratulation of yourselves?* (ASV). Two
things are implied: First, the Galatians at one time had looked upon
Paul's presence among them as grounds for congratulating themselves.
Second, the self-felicitation of the Galatians had ceased, and for no
good reason. The word translated "gratulation" ("blessedness," KJV),
used elsewhere in the New Testament only in Romans 4:6, 9, means
a "declaration of blessedness." Norlie translates it "blessed good will";
Phillips, "that fine spirit"; RSV, "the satisfaction you felt." The NEB
renders the whole question, "Have you forgotten how happy you
thought yourselves in having me with you?"

The latter part of verse 15 shows that their appreciation for the
work of Paul in their midst was once so great that they would have
done anything in their power for him. *For I bear you witness,* he
writes, *that, if possible, ye would have plucked out your eyes and
given them to me* (ASV). This statement often is cited in support of

the view that the "infirmity" mentioned above was a disease of the eyes. Note the KJV rendering, which lends some support to this view by inserting "own" before "eyes." There is, however, no justification for this in the Greek text. This interpretation, therefore, though possible, is probably not correct. The emphasis rests on the word "eyes" — "your very eyes," might express it — and the whole statement is to be taken as simply a graphic description of the ardent and unselfish love of the Galatians. So great was their sense of indebtedness to Paul, they would have been willing to make any sacrifice for him.

But that was long ago. Now the Galatians have undergone a change of attitude. The one they once welcomed as an angel, even as Christ Jesus, they now regard as their enemy. The apostle cannot understand the reason for the change. He asks, therefore, somewhat indignantly, *Am I therefore become your enemy* [i.e., hostile to you] *because I tell you the truth?* (verse 16). Guthrie thinks Paul put the matter like this so as to leave "a loophole" for the Galatians to deny the charge (p. 127). (Burton feels that verse 16 should be punctuated with an exclamation mark: "So that I have become your enemy by telling you the truth!" [p. 244]. Others take it as a simple statement: "So then I have become your enemy by being honest with you.")

When did this telling of the truth occur? Obviously, the reference could not be to statements made in the present letter, for at the time of writing it Paul surely could not have known what its effect would be on his readers. Nor could the reference be to the occasion mentioned in verses 14 and 15; no hostility was expressed then. A more probable view is that Paul is referring to a previous letter which had elicited a negative reaction from the Galatians. This letter, if there was such, has not survived. It is best to understand Paul as referring to things said on a second visit to the Galatians. The whole question is of considerable interest in understanding the chronology of Paul's contacts with the Galatians.

2. *Paul's affection for the Galatians* (verses 17-20). The real reason for the change in the Galatians' attitude is suggested in verse 17, where a third party (the Judaizers) is brought into the argument. *They zealously seek you in no good way* [RSV: *for no good purpose*]; *nay, they desire to shut you out, that ye may seek them* (ASV). Paul, by speaking the truth to his readers, had incurred their suspicion and hostility. His opponents courted their favor, but not sincerely. Their intention was to exclude ("shut out") the Galatian Christians from Paul, that is, to cause a rift between the two. Moffatt: "they want to debar you from us." Phillips: "They would like to see you and me

separated altogether." Their ultimate aim, however, was to turn the affections and interests of the Galatians to themselves. Coneybeare puts it, "that your zeal may be for them alone" (verse 17b).

Paul was distressed that false teachers had found it so easy to steal away the hearts of his readers and make them think of him as their enemy. So in verse 18 he expresses the wish that the ardent devotion which the Galatians had shown for him on his first visit might be continued now that he is separated from them. *But it is good to be zealously sought in a good matter at all times, and not only when I am present with you* (ASV).

The interpretation of this verse is extremely difficult, the main problem being whether it is Paul or the Galatians being "sought." The first part of the verse is slated so generally that it could apply either way. Verse 18b, however, seems to speak of the devotion Paul would like to receive from the Galatians. This consideration leads Ribberbos to conclude that this is the sense of the entire verse. "Paul, thinking of the efforts of the heretical teachers, admits it to be a good and desirable thing to desire the favor and love of the churches. Paul wants these himself also, but only in a good matter. Nor does he want to have it when he is with them, only to be forgotten and rejected by them when he has gone away" (pp. 169, 170). Sanday concludes that it is a mistake to refer the verse exclusively either to Paul or to the Galatians. "The proposition is stated in a general form, so as to cover both" (p. 452).

Paul's concern for the Galatians is so deep that he feels as though he is passing through the pangs of birth in their behalf. *My little children, of whom I travail in birth again until Christ be formed in you* (verse 19). The term of address is a diminutive used frequently by John but only here by Paul. It is expressive of tenderness and affection and is especially appropriate in the context of this verse. The mention of "travail," the word used for birth pains, points up the deep solicitude and painful anxiety of the apostle. The anguish which he endured in bringing the Galatian churches to birth is again being experienced by him because of their present failure.

But Paul's concern is not simply that the Galatians should be intellectually persuaded of and confirmed in the truth of the Gospel. He wants Christ to "be formed in" them. The metaphor is mixed, but the meaning is clear. The verb employed was used in ancient medical writings to describe the formation of an embryo within the womb. Here the thought is of Christ-likeness and the Christ-life being shaped in the believer (cf. 2:20). Weiss interprets the clause to mean "until you have become Christians in whom Christ alone lives" (quoted by Williams, p. 100).

Paul wishes that he could be present with his converts and change the tone of his voice. *I could wish to be present with you now, and to change my tone; for I am perplexed about you* (verse 20, ASV). These words do not mean that Paul regrets what he has said in this letter. If that had been so, he would not have sent it. Rather, they express Paul's confidence that if he could only see the Galatians face to face their differences could be worked out and the voice of blame which sounds throughout this letter would be changed to a voice of praise. His reason for this wish is expressed in the words "for I am perplexed about you" (verse 20b, ASV). The literal meaning of the Greek verb is "to be without a way in which to go." It then comes to mean "to be puzzled," "to be at a loss" what to think or what to do. Moffatt translates it here, "I am at my wits' end about you!" Taylor: "at this distance I frankly don't know what to do."

FOR FURTHER STUDY

1. Learn what you can about Paul's "infirmity in the flesh."

CHAPTER 7

The Truth of the Gospel:

The Allegorical Illustration

(Galatians 4:21-31)

The apostle, having set forth his case by a carefully reasoned argument and having entreated his readers on the basis of their mutual affection, closes this section of the letter with an illustration drawn from biblical history. Burton thinks that this paragraph is brought in as a kind of afterthought. Ridderbos, on the other hand, supposes that Paul intended all along to include it, and that he deliberately placed it here to serve as the "climax and capstone" of the entire discussion of the law and the Gospel.

Paul has been severely criticized for his handling of the story alluded to in these verses. It is contended that he reads too much into the meanings of mere words and that the argument generally is too subtle to be convincing. The whole paragraph, we are told, is a typical instance of rabbinical interpretation. In answer to this criticism at least two things may be said: First, such rabbinical interpretations carried much weight with Paul's readers, accustomed as they were to Jewish methods of treating the Scriptures. As Meyer explains, his intention was "to destroy the influence of the false Apostles with their own weapons, and to root it up out of its own proper soil." Second, and more important, Paul does not use the typical allegorizing method employed by the rabbis. They extracted from historical, biblical narratives principles which were foreign to the events recorded. Contrary to this, Paul cites an Old Testament event the salient features of which point up and illustrate the very essence of his argument.

The primary lesson to be learned from the story is that there are two branches of the Abrahamic family, one physical, the other spiritual. Those whose relation to Abraham is physical are in bondage; those whose relation to Abraham is spiritual are free.

The paragraph may be divided as follows: (1) the historical facts of the case (verses 21-23), (2) the interpretation of the facts (verses

24-27), (3) the application to the readers (verses 28-30), and (4) a concluding statement (verse 31).

I. THE HISTORICAL FACTS (4:21-23).

By their conduct the Galatians had shown a desire (a wish) to be under the law. Paul therefore asks, *Tell me, ye that desire to be under the law, do ye not hear the law?* (verse 21). The tone, which is less tender, more commanding than that of the preceding paragraph, reflects Paul's excitement. The abruptness with which the thought is stated served to arrest the attention of the readers.

"Ye that desire to be under the law" indicates that the Galatians had not yet put themselves under the yoke of legalism but were on the verge of doing so.

There may be a touch of irony in the words "do ye not hear the law?" That is, you who wish so much to be under the law, why do you not listen more attentively to what it says? (In the first part of verse 21 "law" means the Mosaic law; in the latter part of the verse the word is used in the sense of the Pentateuch, of which the Mosaic code was a part.)

Verses 22 and 23 constitute a brief summary of the story by which Paul wishes to illustrate the difference between the law and the Gospel.

The leading facts are these: (1) *Abraham had two sons* (verse 22a). (Actually he had more than two, but it is clear that Ishmael and Isaac are the two in mind.) The point is that Abraham has descendants other than those who come from Isaac, the son of Sarah. (2) These sons were different in *origin* (one [Ishmael] was born of a slave girl and the other [Isaac] was born of a free woman, verse 22b); they were also markedly different in the *circumstances of their birth*. The birth of the slave girl's child was *after the flesh* (verse 23a), that is, there was nothing of miracle about it; his birth was according to the usual course of nature. The child of the free woman was *born through promise* (verse 23b, ASV). That is, there was a miraculous intervention that made possible a birth which was contrary to the course of nature.

II. THE INTERPRETATION OF THE FACTS (4:24-27).

These things, Paul argues, *contain an allegory* (verse 24a, ASV). The Greek word means "to speak allegorically," that is, to express one thing under the figure of another. Some think its sense here is "to have an allegorical meaning." Bruce paraphrases it: "Now this teaches us a spiritual lesson." The apostle does not intend to question the historical truth of the story. That is to say, he does not look upon it as an allegory in itself. He simply regards it as embodying principles which typify the bondage of those who are under law and the liberty of the people of faith.

The two women, Hagar the slave girl and Sarah the free woman, *are [i.e., symbolize or represent] two covenants* (verse 24b, ASV). One covenant derives from mount Sinai, and bears children destined for bondage. This *is [corresponds to] Hagar* (verse 24c, ASV). (The second covenant is not here mentioned but is taken up in verse 26 in the reference to "the Jerusalem that is above.") *Now this Hagar is [stands for, corresponds to] Mount Sinai in Arabia* (verse 25a, ASV). Chrysostom, Luther, and others interpret this to mean that the word "Hagar" in Arabia (i.e., among the Arabs) is another name for Mount Sinai. Those who subscribe to this view usually conclude that Paul learned this fact during his visit in Arabia (Gal. 1:17). An interpretation more widely held today takes the expression to mean "Now this [woman] Hagar *represents* Mount Sinai in Arabia." Williams, however, thinks it is not the word "Hagar" and not the woman as such that Paul has in mind; it is rather the *thought of bondage* suggested by Hagar's name that is here identified with Sinai.

Furthermore, Hagar *answereth [corresponds] to the Jerusalem that now is: for she is in bondage with her children* (verse 25b, (ASV). "The Jerusalem that now is" (present earthly Jerusalem) here stands for the Jewish system, of which it was the center. It is this Jerusalem, here personified, which "is in bondage with her children." There is perhaps a double reference in the word "bondage" — enslavement to Rome and enslavement to the law. The primary reference, however, must be to the bondage of the Mosaic law. Jerusalem's "children," essentially a reference to physical Israel, might include any others who put themselves under the yoke of the Jewish legal system.

Over against "the Jerusalem that now is" Paul sets *the Jerusalem that is above* (verse 26, ASV). This is the heavenly Jerusalem, thought of as the true home of believers in Christ (cf. Phil. 3:20). This Jerusalem, in marked contrast to earthly Jerusalem, is not under bondage to the law but *is free*. That is, it is under the rule of grace. In calling the heavenly Jerusalem *our mother* Paul suggests it is from this source that we derive our life. Just as the earthly Jerusalem was the metropolis ("mother-city") of Judaism, the heavenly Jerusalem is the metropolis ("mother-city") of Christianity.

Verse 27, which is a quotation of Isaiah 54:1, picks up and develops the idea of motherhood which has been introduced in the preceding verse. In its original setting the Isaiah passage describes the restoration and surpassing greatness of the city of Jerusalem after the Exile. The imagery employed is that of a barren wife (Jerusalem) deserted by her husband but eventually (after the Exile) accepted again by him and fruitful in the bearing of children. In Paul's thought the passage has Messianic significance and finds its deepest fulfillment in the growth of the Church. The barren woman corresponds to Sarah, who had no child until late in her life. The woman who has a husband corresponds to Hagar. The point of the quotation is that Sarah, though barren through most of her life, finally became (through Isaac) the mother of more children than Hagar. Applied spiritually, it means that the Christian community (symbolized by Sarah), though in Paul's day small and bereft of the outward glories of Judaism (symbolized by Hagar), is destined for greater fruitfulness and glory.

Before passing on to Paul's application of his allegory, it may be well to summarize the main points of comparison. This may best be done by setting them in parallel columns as follows:

Hagar, the bond woman	Sarah, the free woman
Ishmael, the child after the flesh	Isaac, the child of promise
The old covenant	The new covenant
The earthly Jerusalem	The heavenly Jerusalem

III. THE APPLICATION TO THE READERS (4:28-30).

Verses 28-31 give the application of the allegory. Three points are made. First, we who believe in Christ and depend wholly on him for acceptance with God *as Isaac was, are children of promise* (verse 28, ASV). Just as Isaac was Abraham's son through the fulfillment of a divine promise, so believers owe their standing with God not to physical descent but to the creative word of God. Paul's language shows that he "looked upon the extraordinary birth of Isaac as having its counterpart in the regeneration of men by the Spirit of God" (Hovey, p. 62). Second, now as then the people of promise may expect to be persecuted by those whose descent from Abraham is strictly physical (verse 29). *Born after the flesh* means born in the ordinary course of nature. "Born after the Spirit" means born supernaturally, that is, in accordance with the divine promise which is fulfilled by the power and work of the Spirit of God. Third, the law must give place to the Gospel. Legalistic Judaism must be rejected by the people of faith (verse 30).

IV. CONCLUSION (4:31).

Verse 31 is a summing up of the entire paragraph. We who are believers in Christ, Paul writes, *are not children of a handmaid, but of the freewoman* (ASV). The idea is that those who are the people of faith belong not to a community that is in bondage to legal statutes, but to a community whose relation to God is that of sons and heirs.

FOR FURTHER STUDY

1. Read Genesis 16-18.
2. Read articles on "Hagar," "Ishmael," "Isaac," and "Allegory."

CHAPTER 8

The Life of the Christian:

A Life of Freedom

(Galatians 5:1-15)

The first four chapters of Galatians are decidedly polemical. In them Paul has defended his apostleship (chapters 1 and 2) and has expounded and defended the truth of his Gospel (chapters 3 and 4). The two final chapters breathe the same air of controversy, but their emphasis is somewhat different. Whereas the earlier chapters have stressed doctrine, these focus attention on duty. There are, to be sure, great doctrinal utterances in chapters 4 and 5, but the drift of the discussion concerns the practical issues of the Gospel rather than a theoretical exposition of it. The first part of Galatians (especially chapters 3 and 4) has unfolded the method of gaining a right relationship with God; the section we are now to study urges upon the readers the performance of those duties which grow out of a right relationship with God. Paul's treatment of these duties becomes a sort of exposition of the nature of the Christian life. The impression left on the readers is that it is (1) a life of freedom (5:1-15), (2) a life controlled by the Spirit (5:16-26), and (3) a life of love (6:1-10). The first of these concepts is the subject of this chapter. The other two will be considered in the following chapters.

The idea of freedom has pervaded much of the earlier portions of Galatians. Indeed, there are those who see this as the motif of the entire epistle. Viewed in this fashion, chapters 1 and 2 set forth "the apostle of freedom"; chapters 3 and 4, "the gospel of freedom"; and chapters 5 and 6, "the life of freedom."

There are two perils which threaten the Christian's freedom in Christ. One (treated in verses 1-12) is legalism. The other (treated in verses 13-15) is license. The former is a denial of freedom, the latter a perversion of it. Both are to be earnestly resisted.

I. FREEDOM VERSUS LEGALISM (5:1-12).

In verses 1-12 Paul urges his readers to treasure their freedom and never again to permit themselves to be enslaved. The discussion is woven about (1) an assertion (verse 1a), (2) a command (verse 1b), (3) a warning (verses 2-6), and (4) an appeal (verses 7-12).

1. *The assertion* (verse 5:1a). Verse 1, which should be read in a translation other than KJV, is in two distinct parts. The first part, which many look upon as the final statement of the preceding paragraph, is transitional. It summarizes the argument which has preceded and prepares the reader for the exhortation which follows. *For freedom did Christ set us free* (verse 1a, ASV). The manner of expression may be intended to emphasize the completeness of the liberty believers have in Christ. Weymouth's rendering brings this out: "Christ has made us completely free." However, it is probably better to follow the ASV. The thought then is that Christ has liberated us *for the purpose of freedom.*

The freedom of which the apostle is thinking is that which has been under discussion in the preceding chapter, namely, freedom from the law of Moses. This of course does not mean that the Christian is free from the moral demands of the law. It does mean that he is freed from its curse (3:13, 24), and from the deadening power of its rule.

2. *The command* (verse 1b). Having asserted the freedom which Christ has gained for the Christian, Paul now charges his readers to cling to it. His command is stated positively and negatively. *Stand fast therefore, and be not entangled again in a yoke of bondage* (ASV). "Stand fast," which translates a verb having intensive force, suggests a tenacious stand in and for freedom. The word "therefore" shows that this is a duty growing out of the fact that Christ has set us free. "Entangled" is the rendering of a Greek verb whose literal meaning is "to be held in." In this context the suggestion is that the readers are in danger of being held in, that is, restrained by a yoke. The English word "entangled," which brings to mind the idea of a net or a cord, fails to express this imagery. But either way, the thought is clear: Do not let anyone make slaves of you again.

3. *The warning* (verses 2-6). Paul's language at this point becomes somewhat stern, almost indignant. Speaking with the full weight of his apostolic authority (verse 2a), he warns his readers that they must choose, once for all, between Christ and the law. The thought may be summarized as follows: The acceptance of circumcision is tantamount to full surrender to the principle of legalism, and those who receive it

in order to gain acceptance with God obligate themselves to obey the whole law. Circumcision is in essence a kind of pledge to live by the rule of the law, and the law cannot be fragmented. It must be taken as a whole. Those who are committed to the law-method of salvation must of necessity make this their only hope of justification. In so doing they cut themselves off from Christ, for there can be no combining the Gospel of grace and the law of Moses. To accept the one as grounds for justification is to reject the other. True Christians, therefore, trust Christ alone for salvation and eagerly await the fulfillment of their hope (the verdict of final acquittal) through the Spirit (not through the law) and by faith (not by works). They realize that in union with Christ faith working through love is all that matters.

A threefold warning is given the readers: First, if they receive circumcision (as a means of gaining acceptance with God) they will lose the benefits of Christ's work. *Behold, I Paul say unto you, that, if ye receive circumcision, Christ will profit you nothing* (verse 2, ASV). The general sense is that in receiving circumcision (as a condition of salvation) the readers put themselves in a position in which Christ will be of no advantage to them. He is of advantage only to those who trust him exclusively. The opening words ("Behold, I Paul," etc.) emphasize the apostle's authority and point up the significance and importance of the statement which follows. The NEB captures the spirit of it by rendering it, "Mark my words: I, Paul. . . ." "If ye receive circumcision" is the rendering of a Greek construction which implies that the readers, though considering it, have not yet yielded to the demand that they be circumcised. "Christ will profit you nothing" (Bruce: "will be of no use to you") implies that law and grace are contradictory methods of salvation and that there can be no compromise between, nor combination of, them. Salvation comes either through obedience to law (circumcision) or through faith in Christ. It cannot be through both Christ and circumcision.

Second, if they receive circumcision (as a means of gaining acceptance with God) they bind themselves to keep the whole law. *Yea, I testify again to every man that receiveth circumcision, that he is a debtor [is under obligation] to do the whole law* (verse 3, ASV). The reasoning is that the law is a unit, and to confess that one is obligated to obey a part of it is to admit that he is obligated to obey all of it (cf. 3:10; James 2:10). The Judaizers apparently had not proposed that the Galatians keep the whole law, but Paul contends that the acceptance of circumcision is in principle a surrender to the entire legalistic system. Paul, fearing that the Galatians were about to take this decisive step, urges them to consider its far-reaching implications. The depth of his feeling on this matter is revealed in the use of the verb "testify," which means not simply "to bear witness" but "to affirm solemnly."

Third, if they receive circumcision (as a means of gaining acceptance with God) they leave Christianity and join Judaism. *Ye are severed from Christ, ye who would be [i.e., who are trying to be] justified by the law; ye are fallen away from grace* (verse 4). This verse states in stronger, more vivid language the thought of verse 2. The Greek word for "severed" ("become of no effect," KJV) basically means "to render inoperative," "to bring to nothing," "to render null and void." Paul uses it approximately twenty-five times in his writings, but elsewhere in the New Testament it occurs only twice (Luke 13:7; Heb. 2:14). The KJV uses nineteen different terms to translate the word: "destroy," "abolish," "make without effect," "bring to nought," "put away," and so forth. In the present passage the versions exhibit considerable variety in rendering it. Conybeare has "you are cut off from Christ"; Goodspeed, "have finished with Christ"; NEB, "your relation with Christ is completely severed"; Moffatt, "ye are done with Christ." The thought is that a reversion to the law means that one's relation to Christ is cancelled. All connection with Him has been severed. Christ must be everything to a person or He is nothing. The idea is further elaborated in the closing words of the verse: "ye are fallen away from grace." "Grace" is used here as the opposite of law (works). It is a principle of life, a method of justification. The essence of it is, "By seeking to be justified by works of law, you have fallen away from, that is, have renounced, the way of justification by grace." The passage therefore really has nothing to say about the modern idea of "falling from grace." Paul was thinking about two methods of salvation, one by law, the other by grace. To turn to law is to turn away from grace. Moffatt: "you have deserted grace."

The attitude of those who are truly saved is expressed in verse 5: *For we [emphatic] through the Spirit by faith wait for the hope of righteousness* (ASV). That is to say, true Christians look forward to being accepted by God on the ground of faith, not of law. The word rendered "wait for" means "to wait eagerly," "to look forward to." The idea of expectancy is prominent. "Hope," which here denotes the object of hope, is defined as "righteousness." This latter word speaks of right standing or acceptance with God through Christ. The reference is to the final verdict of acquittal at the judgment of God. There is a sense in which righteousness is bestowed upon the believer at the time of his conversion (Rom. 9:30), but the suggestion here is that the complete possession of it is not ours until the end of the age. In similar fashion, Paul teaches elsewhere that we hope for adoption as sons (Rom. 8:23), though in a sense we already have attained this sonship (cf. Gal. 3:26; 4:5). Similarly, he speaks of the hope of salvation in 1 Thessalonians 5:4.

Verse 6, which sums up this part of the discussion, expresses the central thrust of Galatians. The essence of it is that if a man is in union with Christ Jesus, circumcision means nothing and the lack of it means nothing; all that matters is faith which finds expression in love. Faith, in Paul's thinking, is a complete committal of one's self to Christ.

4. *The appeal* (verses 7-12). In the preceding section (verses 1-6) Paul has dealt with circumcision and its implications for his readers. In these verses (7-12) he is concerned not with the rite of circumcision but with those who were preaching it. Reference is made to their hindering (verse 7), their persuading (verse 8), their troubling (verse 10), and their unsettling (verse 12) the Galatians. The mood throughout is much like that of 1:6-10, and several words and concepts are common to the two passages. The style is very abrupt, the thought shifting quickly from subject to subject. The paragraph closes in a vein of severe irony.

The apostle begins with an acknowledgment that the Galatians had made a noble start. Using the imagery of a race, he writes, *Ye were running well* (verse 7a, ASV). Goodspeed: "You were making such progress!" The language suggests the eagerness and the persistency which had marked the beginning of their Christian lives.

But something had happened to change all of this. *Who hindered you,* asks Paul, *that ye should not obey the truth?* (verse 7b, ASV). The question is not raised in order to elicit information. It is intended rather to arrest the attention of the readers and cause them to consider what is happening to them. "Hindered" translates a verb used in ancient times of cutting into a road or of breaking it up so as to impede the advance of an army. In the present passage the word suggests that somebody had thrown an obstacle in the course of the Galatians and thus had hindered their advance in the Christian life. The reference is to the Judaizing teachers whom Paul has opposed throughout this letter.

Verse 8 is in part the answer to Paul's question: *This persuasion [no longer to obey the truth] came not of him that calleth you* (ASV). That is, pressures leading you to disobey the truth cannot be from

God. "Persuasion," which translates a Greek word cognate with the verb "obey" in the preceding verse, probably refers to the persuasive talk of the Judaizers. It may perhaps be a general term for all of the influences and pressures to which the Galatians were being subjected. "Him that calleth you" is God.

Verse 9 contains a proverbial statement which illustrates the danger of the persuasion brought to bear on the Galatians. *A little leaven leaveneth the whole lump* (cf. 1 Cor. 5:6). Leaven, a symbol frequently found both in the Old Testament and in the New, ordinarily (though not always) denotes evil. The "little leaven" may refer either to the false teachers or to the erroneous doctrine propagated by them. Perhaps both ideas are here, for one cannot be separated from the other. The sense is quite clear: The teachers of error may be few in number, but unless something is done to check their influence they soon will ruin the whole Christian community.

In spite of Paul's distress over the situation, he expresses his confidence in the majority of his readers. *I have confidence to you-ward in the Lord, that ye will be none otherwise minded* (verse 10a, ASV). The pronoun "I" is emphatic and appears to be set over against "he that troubleth you" (verse 10b). "In the Lord" (ASV) suggests that Paul's confidence stems from his relationship to Christ. The TCNT: "I, through my union with the Lord, am persuaded."

That of which the apostle is confident is that the Galatian Christians "will be none otherwise minded." That is to say, he is confident that they will share his opinion on the things under discussion, namely that the influence exerted by the Judaizers is a leaven of evil which does not come of God and that it is a serious threat to the spiritual well-being of the churches.

Paul's convictions concerning those troubling the Galatians are just as firm. He is persuaded that *he that troubleth you shall bear his judgment, whosoever he be* (verse 10b, ASV). Some think the apostle uses the singular form ("he that troubleth you") to designate some particular individual, possibly the leader of the Judaizing teachers. It is not necessary, however, to draw this conclusion. The singular may be used only for the sake of emphasis. In that case, all Paul means is that anyone who is the occasion of spiritual distress to the Galatians will be judged of (i.e., punished by) God. Emphasis is further brought out by the addition of "whosoever he be."

Verse 11 implies that the false teachers were accusing Paul of inconsistency in his own preaching. They claimed that Paul did not always oppose circumcision but sometimes, when it was convenient to him, preached it himself. The grounds of this accusation may have been (a) his having Timothy to submit to circumcision (Acts 16:3) and (b) his indifference to circumcision in the case of Jews (cf. 1 Cor. 7:18). From this Paul's opponents argued that the apostle adjusted his preaching to his audience and to their circumstances.

The question in the first part of verse 11 is Paul's answer to this charge of duplicity. It is introduced very abruptly and shows the deep agitation of the apostle's mind. *But I [emphatic], brethren, if I [as the Judaizers claim] still preach circumcision, why am I still persecuted?* (verse 11a, ASV). The question implies that Paul's persecution was for preaching anti-legalism. "All of my sufferings," he seems to say, "may be traced to my fidelity to the Gospel of Christ and to my insistence that righteousness comes by faith alone. It is illogical, therefore, for the Judaists to persecute me and at the same time allege that I preach their doctrine. The cross is the stone over which they stumble, but if I (as they say) preach circumcision, *then hath the stumbling-block of the cross been done away?* (verse 11b, ASV).

From this verse we may gather that circumcision occupied the same place in the teaching of the Judaizers that the cross of Christ had in the teaching of Paul. Paul asserts that he could not possibly have been preaching both circumcision and the cross. The two are contradictory and mutually exclusive systems. One might accept one or the other; he could not possibly hold to both.

The KJV interprets verse 12 as an expression of Paul's desire that the teachers of error would cut themselves off from the Galatian Christians. Phillips' rendering also conveys this meaning: "I wish those who are so eager to cut your bodies would cut themselves off from you altogether." However, all of the ancient Greek interpreters and the majority of modern interpreters prefer a different understanding of the text. The TCNT conveys this sense: *I could even wish that the people who are unsettling you would go further still and mutilate themselves.* Rendered in this fashion, the verse is an expression of bitter irony revealing the depth of the apostle's indignation against those who slandered him and troubled his converts. The words do not mean that he actually wants his opponents to mutilate themselves. He simply uses mocking satire to point up the logical issue of the Judaizers' veneration for circumcision. If a fleshly rite is so meaningful, Paul suggests, why stop with circumcision? Why not go on and "make eunuchs of themselves" (NEB)? The words may contain an allusion to the self-mutilation practiced by the priests of Cybele, whose worship had one of its most important centers in Galatia.

II. Freedom versus license (5:13-15).

The previous paragraph (verses 1-12), in which believers are urged to stand fast in the freedom which Christ has won for them, warns of the danger of losing Christian freedom through a return to legalism. In the present passage (verses 13-15) the opposite danger is discussed. Here the apostle shows that freedom may be abused, that it may be perverted, by turning it into license. This also is to be resisted earnestly.

There are always some who in the name of liberty practice moral and spiritual anarchy, and apparently there were at least a few people among the Galatians guilty of doing this. They may have seized upon the anti-legalistic element in Paul's teaching as an excuse for their dissolute behavior. Paul teaches that liberty is not an excuse for self-indulgence.

The passage, somewhat like the preceding, contains an assertion (verse 13a), an appeal (verses 13b, 14), and a warning (verse 15).

1. *The assertion* (verse 13a). *For ye, brethren, were called for freedom* (asv). "For" indicates that this statement has a connection with what has gone before. It is as though the apostle were saying, "I cannot but feel deep indignation when I think of the work of the Judaizers, for you were called to freedom in Christ." The use of the word "brethren" shows Paul's warm affection for his readers. "Called for freedom" means called with a view to freedom in Christ.

2. *The appeal* (verses 13b, 14). The freedom of the Galatians is real, and must be treasured and guarded. On the other hand, they must not in the name of liberty give themselves to sinful practices. *Only use not your freedom for an occasion to the flesh* (verse 13b, asv). The word "only" is perhaps a reflection of Paul's anxious fear that some of the Galatians may already have been guilty of this. "The flesh" stands not simply for the physical body, but for the whole sinful nature of man. The neb interprets it to mean "the lower nature." Burton defines it as "that element of man's nature which is opposed to goodness, and makes for evil" (p. 292). The Greek word for "occasion," found only in Paul in the New Testament, was used by the ancients of a base of operation in war. If this is the imagery of the word in the present passage, the suggestion is that liberty must never become a base from which our sinful natures lead us to disobey God. Most interpreters, however, understand the thought to be that Christian liberty must never become a pretext, an excuse, for self-indulgence (cf. C. B. Williams' translation).

As a preventive to such self-indulgence the apostle urges his readers *by love* to *serve* [lit., "render slave service to"] *one another* (verse 13c). The ASV renders it, "But through love be servants one to another." Paul has warned his readers against one kind of slavery (i.e., legalism) and has urged them to maintain their freedom. Now he reminds them that there is another kind of slavery that is not only permissible, but is to be desired and practiced. It is not a bondage to the law, nor to any system or institution. Rather, it is a bondage of love to one another. Conybeare expresses it best: "but rather enslave yourselves to one another by the bondage of love." The tense of the verb is present, suggesting a continuing activity.

Paul enforces this command by quoting a great moral principle which interestingly enough is embedded in the very heart of the Mosaic law (Lev. 19:18). *For the whole law is fulfilled in one word, even in this: Thou shalt love thy neighbor as thyself* (verse 14, ASV). Luther comments that in verbal form this statement "is very brief; but in act and fact it is broader, longer, deeper, and higher than the whole world."

The meaning of the verse turns on the interpretation of the verb "fulfilled." It may, for instance, mean that the whole law, viewed as a unit, is *summed up* in the command to love (cf. TCNT). That is to say, this command embodies in itself man's whole duty to man. On the other hand, the word "fulfilled" may mean that the whole law *has been brought to perfection* in the command to love. In this interpretation the idea is that the law finds its truest statement, its crowning expression in the command to love. A third possibility is that the reference is to *fulfillment by deed*. That is, the whole law is summmarily fulfilled (performed) in the keeping of this one command. Burton, who prefers this interpretation, paraphrases as follows: "The whole law stands fully obeyed in (obedience to) one word" (p. 295). This is the interpretation which Paul gives in Romans 13:8, where a similar statement occurs. The tense of the verb points to a completed act having permanent results.

3. *The warning* (verse 15). Obviously the Galatians have not been living by this law of love, so Paul issues a warning: *But if ye bite and devour one another, take heed that ye be not consumed one of another* (verse 15, ASV). Burton says that the three verbs ("bite," "devour," and "consume") "suggest wild animals engaged in deadly struggle" (p. 297). In the Greek the first two are in the present tense, suggesting continual or habitual activity. The tense of the third word is aorist, implying utter destruction. The TEV: "But if you act like

animals, hurting and harming each other, then watch out, or you will completely destroy one another."

For Further Study

1. Study articles on "Law," "Freedom," "Grace," "Justification," and "Flesh" in a Bible dictionary.

2. Read Galatians again, marking each reference to these words in the epistle.

3. Read Maclaren's sermon on Galatians 5:6, entitled "What Makes a Christian: Circumcision or Faith?"

CHAPTER 9

The Life of the Christian:

A Life Controlled by the Spirit

(Galatians 5:16-26)

In the first half of Chapter 5 Paul has represented the Christian life as a life of freedom. In developing this theme he has shown that freedom is imperilled on the one hand by legalism and on the other by license. True freedom, Paul has explained, expresses itself not in self-indulgence but in loving service to others.

But the question arises, How is such a life possible? That is, how can one avoid the self-indulgence of libertinism without resorting to the bondage of legalism? The answer is set out in 5:16-26, the passage which we must now consider. Here the Christian life is portrayed as a life regulated by the Spirit of God. Burton appropriately comments that this kind of life is by no means a middle course between legalism and license, but is "a highway above them both, a life of freedom from statutes, of faith and love" (p. 302).

The passage has four divisions: The first contains an exhortation to walk by the Spirit (verses 16-18); the second, a listing of the works of the flesh (verses 19-21); the third, a description of the fruit of the Spirit (verses 22-24); and the fourth, a summary (verses 25, 26).

I. An exhoration to walk by the spirit (5:16-18).

The best way of opposing the evil impulses of our lower nature is to yield ourselves to the control of the Spirit. *But I say, Walk by ["in,"* kjv] *the Spirit, and ye shall not fulfil the lust of the flesh* (verse 16, asv). The introductory words, "But I say," are intended to mark the importance of the words that follow. To "walk by the Spirit" is to lead a life governed by the power of the Spirit (cf. 5:5, 18, 25). The verb, which Paul uses more than thirty times, is here in the present tense and speaks of habitual action: "Keep on walking, etc."

When this is done, writes Paul, *ye shall not fulfil the lust of the flesh* (verse 16b). "Fulfil" translates a Greek word different from that similarly rendered in verse 14. A somewhat literal meaning is, "You will not accomplish." Some of the versions use "gratify." The form of the statement in Greek is especially emphatic: "you will *never* gratify, etc." It does not express a command (as in rsv) but a strong assurance or promise that the believer whose life is Spirit-directed will be able to resist and conquer the lust of the flesh. "Lust" simply means desire, but in this context the word has a connotation of evil. Moffatt has "passions"; tcnt, "cravings." "Flesh" is not to be interpreted as a reference merely to bodily appetites. The word stands for all the tendencies and impulses which lead to wrong conduct. Phillips and the neb use the expression "lower nature"; Bruce, "old nature."

The opposition of flesh and Spirit is explained in verse 17: *For the flesh lusteth against the Spirit, and the Spirit against the flesh; for these are contrary the one to the other; that ye may not do the things that ye would.* The conflict here thus described is a fierce and unrelenting warfare to establish dominion over man's soul in the expression: "for these are contrary one to the other." The verb has a connotation of hostility, the root idea being that of two things set one against the other. Bruce brings this out in translation: "they are diametrically opposed to each other."

The result of this fierce opposition between the Spirit and the flesh is that the Christian finds himself acting differently from the way he would like to act: "So that ye cannot do the things that ye would."

Some (Duncan, for example) interpret this to mean that the Spirit counteracts the flesh to prevent our carrying out its evil impulses. On the other hand, there are those who take the opposite view. Hovey, for example, explains the statement to mean that "the opposition of sinful desire arrests the better choice 'so that' it is not carried into effect" (p. 69). Still others understand the meaning to be that evil impulses are restrained by the Spirit; good impulses, by the flesh. Burton, who is a proponent of this view, sums it up: "Does the man choose evil, the Spirit opposes him; does he choose good, the flesh hinders him" (p. 302). Romans 7:15-23 provides a good commentary on the statement.

II. THE WORKS OF THE FLESH (5:19-21).

Verses 16 and 17 have affirmed the conflict between the Spirit and the flesh (the lower nature). Now the apostle enumerates their respective manifestations. The works of the flesh are listed in verses 19-21; the fruit of the Spirit, in verses 22-26. The "works" of the flesh are the outward expressions of the lust (cravings) of the flesh (cf. verse 16). Bruce interprets the word to mean "activities." *Now the works of the flesh* [the lower nature] *are manifest* (verse 19a). That is, they are evident and well-known. Perhaps the meaning is that they are open for all to see, in contrast to the hiddenness of the lust of the flesh (verse 16). The TCNT: "The sins of our earthly nature are unmistakeable." The list, which is representative but not exhaustive, may be divided in various ways. For instance, a divison often suggested groups them under sins of impurity (the first three), sins connected with idolatry (the fourth and fifth), sins of temper (the next eight), and sins which have to do with drunkenness and its accompaniments (the last two).

1. *Sins of impurity: fornication, uncleanness, lasciviousness* (verse 19b, ASV). The Greek word for "fornication" originally denoted prostitution, but it came eventually to be the most general term for illicit sexual relations. The word rendered "uncleanness" was used by some of the ancient Greek writers of the uncleanness of a sore or wound. In the Septuagint it denotes both ceremonial and moral impurity. In the New Testament, however, the term is used almost exclusively of moral impurity. Most of its occurrences are in Paul. In the present passage it probably has a somewhat broader significance than the word for fornication and signifies any kind of sexual sin. The TCNT has "unchastity." "Lasciviousness" translates a Greek word meaning "wantonness," "debauchery," "lewdness." In this place it has special reference to "wantonness in sexual relations" (Burton, p. 306). Williams interprets the word as "open shamelessness" (p. 124). Sanday understands it to mean "flagrant breaches of public decency" (p. 458).

2. *Sins connected with pagan religion: idolatry and witchcraft* (verse 20a). The former word has to do with the worship of false gods. The latter term, from which the English "pharmacy" is derived, translates a Greek word which originally meant "a drug" or, more generally, "the use of drugs." It came to denote "witchcraft," probably because witches made use of drugs. In the present passage it denotes witchcraft, sorcery, or any kind of magic art.

3. *Sins of temper: enmities, strife, jealousies, wraths, factions, divisions, parties, envyings"* (verses 20b, 21a ASV). These eight sins, which have their root in a loveless heart, all suggest conflict. "Enmities," which signifies hostility in any form, strikes the keynote of the group. It might have been suggested by the preceding reference to sorcery, which often was directed against persons. "Strife" denotes wrangling, dissension, and discord. The NEB: "a contentious temper." "Jealousies"

is a term suggesting rivalry and envy. "Wraths" has to do with out-bursts of anger and hostility. The NEB: "fits of rage." The word ren-dered "factions" may refer either to self-seeking (cf. RSV, "selfishness") or to party spirit (cf. TCNT, "rivalries"). The word for "divisions" may also mean "dissensions" (TCNT, NEB). The literal meaning is "a stand-ing apart." The word for "parties" (KJV, "heresies"), which is similar in meaning to the one which immediately precedes it, denotes "divisions organised into parties" (Sanday, p. 458). Barclay calls it "crystallized dissension" (p. 53). Bruce uses the term "party-spirit." "Envyings," a word suggesting ill-will, refers here to specific expressions of envious desire. The term is somewhat stronger than, but not radically different from, the word translated "jealousies" in verse 20.

4. *Sins of drunkenness: drunkenness, revellings, and such like* (verse 21a). "Revellings" has to do with carousings, both public and private. The reference here may be to the public festivals connected with the worship of the gods. The words "and such like" show that the apostle has not made an exhaustive list.

In the latter part of verse 21 Paul warns that those *who practise such things shall not inherit [i.e., will have no share in] the kingdom of God* (ASV). Similar statements are in 1 Corinthians 6:9, 10 and Ephesians 5:5.

III. THE FRUIT OF THE SPIRIT (5:22-26).

These verses are set over against what has been said about the works of the flesh. Weymouth: "The Spirit, on the other hand, brings a harvest of love, joy," etc. Hunter observes that the word for "harvest" (KJV, "fruit") "suggests that these lovely virtues are the *outflowering* of the indwelling Spirit of God" (p. 39). The nine virtues named are usually thought of as falling into three groups, as follows:

1. *First group: love, joy,* and *peace* (verse 22). These three virtues, like all the rest, have their source in God and cannot be maintained apart from Him. "Love," which translates *agape*, properly stands at the head of the list. In this context it refers mainly to love for one's fellow man. Barclay defines it as "unconquerable benevolence" (p. 54). Hunter interprets it to mean "caring" for other people. The word for "joy" is used in the Bible ordinarily of joy that has its basis in religion, that is, is "grounded in conscious relationship to God" (Burton, p. 314). The word appears only here in Galatians. It is questioned whether "peace" here means the inner peace based upon a conscious-ness of a right relation with God, or a condition of peaceableness toward men. Burton decides for the former and translates it "tranquility

of mind" (p. 314). This appears to be the better way of interpreting it.

2. *Second group: longsuffering, kindness, goodness* (verse 22, ASV).

3. *Third Group: faithfulness, meekness, self-control* (verses 22, 23). "Faithfulness" denotes trustworthiness or fidelity in relation to others. It is the same word which in most places in the New Testament is translated "faith"; however, the context in which it is here used justifies the translation of KJV, ASV, and RSV. Weymouth has "good faith." "Meekness" has been defined as the fruit of humility. It connotes an attitude toward others which results from a proper estimate of ourselves. It includes the notions of submissiveness to God and gentleness toward, or consideration of, others. "Self-control" refers to the mastery of all our appetites and passions.

Paul caps this catalogue of the fruit of the Spirit by asserting that *against such there is no law* (verse 23b). Burton calls this "an understatement . . . for rhetorical effect," and explains that the statement is tantamount to an "emphatic assertion that these things fully meet the requirements of the law" (p. 318). Where they are present there is, then, no need for the restraints of law. Further evidence of this is given in verse 24: *Now those who belong to Christ Jesus* [in contrast to those under the law] *have crucified the lower nature with its passions and appetites* (Weymouth). "Have crucified" refers to the time of their conversion. The tense of the verb (aorist) may stress the finality of the act.

IV. THE SUMMARY (5:25, 26).

Since the flesh with its passions and desires has been crucified, we must therefore see to it that in actual practice our conduct conforms to this fact. *If we live by the Spirit, by the Spirit let us also walk* (verse 25, ASV). To "live by the Spirit" is to derive our life from him. To "walk" by the Spirit means to order our lives by His rule and control. The word translated "walk," which is not the same as that used in verse 16, conveys the thought of making progress on a journey or moving toward a goal. The root idea of the word is to walk in a straight line. The general import of the apostle's appeal is that those who live by the Spirit, that is, derive their life from Him, are to give evidence of this by having a life which is Spirit controlled.

The section closes with an earnest appeal: *Let us not become vainglorious, provoking one another, envying one another* (verse 26, ASV). Life in the Spirit is a life of love, joy, peace, and so forth; but it is not a life exempt from temptation. This verse names three sins as examples of things against which we must be on our guard. "Vainglorious" (RSV:

"self-conceit") denotes a departure from the humility which should characterize the Spirit-directed life. "Provoking" indicates an attitude of combat. The NEB: "challenging one another to rivalry." This also is contrary to the Spirit-directed life. "Envying" refers to feelings of jealousy.

FOR FURTHER STUDY

1. Read Galatians, marking each reference to the Holy Spirit.

2. In several brief statements summarize the main teachings of the epistle concerning the Spirit.

3. Write out briefly your own definition of each of the works of the flesh. Compare this list with James 3:13-16.

4. Compare the fruit of the Spirit with what James says about the wisdom which comes from above (James 3:17, 18).

5. Maclaren has sermons on "Walk in the Spirit" (Gal. 5:16), and "The Fruit of the Spirit" (Gal. 5:22, 23).

6. Spurgeon has two sermons on the materials covered in this Chapter. See his *Treasury of the New Testament*.

7. William Barclay's *Flesh and Spirit* would be helpful reading.

CHAPTER 10

The Life of the Christian:

A Life of Love

(Galatians 6:1-10)

Paul has shown the Christian life to be one of liberty (5:1-15) and Spirit-control (5:16-26). In the present passage (6:1-10) he portrays the Christian life as a life of love. Previously, love has been mentioned as a characteristic of saving faith (5:6), as the channel through which Christians are to serve one another (5:13), as the fulfillment of the law (5:14), and as a fruit of the Spirit (5:22). The word itself is not used in the passage now under consideration, but the various actions which are described as obviously the kinds of deeds which love will prompt one to perform.

The discussion concerns the restoration of those who have fallen into sin (verse 1), the bearing of one another's burdens (verses 2-5), the support of those engaged in Christian teaching (verses 6-8), and doing good toward all (verses 9, 10).

I. THE RESTORATION OF THOSE WHO SIN (6:1).

The last verse of Chapter 5 makes reference to those who, while professing to live by the Spirit, are characterized by pride, jealousy, and combativeness. The opening verse of Chapter 6, which stands in striking contrast to that, describes the attitude and conduct of the truly spiritual person. *Brethren, even if a man be overtaken in any trespass, ye who are spiritual, restore such a one in a spirit of gentleness* (verse 1a, ASV). This is clearly an amplification of the injunction given in 5:25 — "If we live by the Spirit, by the Spirit let us also walk" (ASV). The affectionate term of address ("Brethren") serves to remind the readers that they and Paul are all members of one spiritual family. The conditional clause, introduced by "even if," is tactfully stated as no more than a possible contingency. The word "overtaken" suggests the idea of a sudden and overpowering temptation, and so tends to palliate the guilt of the sinning person. (Compare the NEB:

"If a man should do something wrong, my brothers, on a sudden impulse.") However, it is probably better to see in the Greek word the idea of being "caught in the very act of doing something wrong" (C. B. Williams). In this reading of the text stress is laid on the reality of the offender's guilt. The 'literal meaning of the word for "trespass" is "a falling beside." In KJV it is translated "trespass" (nine times), "offence" (seven times), "sin" (three times), "fall" (two times), and "fault" (here and in James 5:16).

Those who are "spiritual" are to "restore such an one in the spirit of meekness." The "spiritual" are those who live by the Spirit, walk by the Spirit, and exhibit in their lives the fruit of the Spirit. The word for "restore" was used in ancient times of the setting of broken bones, of the mending of nets (Matt. 4:21), and so on. The idea here is that we are to deal with our Christian brothers, even those who have sinned, in a constructive manner. The TEV translates it "set him right"; Phillips, "set him back on the right path." The tense of the verb is present, suggesting not a single act but a process.

The manner in which the word of restoration is to be carried out is defined by two expressions. First, it is to be done in a "spirit of meekness." This refers to an attitude of gentleness, humility, and consideration. Second, it is to be done with full awareness of one's own weaknesses and liability to sin: *considering thyself, lest thou also be tempted* (verse 1b). The use of the singular points up that self-examination is always an individual matter.

II. THE BEARING OF ONE ANOTHER'S BURDENS (6:25).

Another expression of love is the Christian's willingness to take upon himself the burdens of others. *Bear ye one another's burdens, and so fulfil the law of Christ* (verse 2). The injunction is general enough to include burdens of any kind, but the primary reference is to the burdens involved in the case of a fallen brother (verse 1). No burdens are so painful and none so pathetic as are the burdens of a guilty conscience. "Bear" translates a present tense verb, suggesting that we are to make a practice of mutual burden-bearing. The last clause shows that in this manner we will *fulfil* [carry out] *the* [intent of] *the law of Christ.* "The law of Christ" may mean the moral teachings promulgated by Christ. But the expression probably is intended as a contrast to the legalistic system promulgated by the Judaizers. Their system involved submission to a code; the law of Christ involves submission to a person.

Pride and conceit will prevent one from being a burden-bearer.

Therefore the apostle, seeking to remove this obstacle, adds the statement of verse 3: *"For if a man thinketh himself to be something when he is nothing, he deceiveth himself"* (ASV). The final verb of the sentence, which occurs nowhere else in the New Testament, suggests the filling of the mind with fantasies, persuading oneself of the existence of something which has no reality.

Paul teaches that one must test his own work, not by what his brother has failed to do, but by what he knows is his own duty and responsibility. *But let each man prove his own work, and then shall he have his glorying in regard of himself alone, and not of his neighbor* (verse 4, ASV). One who conscientiously does this will have very little ground for boasting. If, however, his manner of life can indeed stand the test of such an examination, "he will have something to boast about on his own account, and not in comparison with his fellows" (Moffatt). It should be observed that this examination is an examination of one's "own" work. It is an individual responsibility. The word for "prove" was used of the testing of metals to determine their purity. Here, the reference is to the testing of moral worth.

Verse 5 on the surface appears to be a contradiction of verse 2, but the words translated "burden" in the two verses are different. [Compare RSV: "burdens," verse 2; "load," verse 6.] In verse 2 the Greek word denotes a crushing weight. Verse 5 employs a word which was used of a soldier's pack. Phillips: "For everyone must 'shoulder his own pack'." The reference is to those responsibilities of life which cannot be shared by another and for which a man will be accountable to God at the judgment. Burton interprets verse 5 as referring to the burden of one's own "weakness and sin." "It is the man who knows he has a burden of his own," he explains, "that is willing to bear his fellow's burden" (p. 334).

III. THE SUPPORT OF CHRISTIAN TEACHERS (6:6-8).

These verses discuss another special instance of burden-bearing on the part of believers: *But let him that is taught in the word communicate unto him that teacheth in all good things* (verse 6, ASV). "Him that teacheth" is the person who is devoting his full time to the work of teaching. The word translated "communicate" in general denoted "to share" or "to be a partner" in a thing or with a person. Here it is said that those who receive instruction from Christian teachers are to share with them "in all good things." Paul was thinking mainly, but perhaps not solely, of things material. Ramsay speaks of the importance of such a command as this in view of the fact that pagan people did not receive instruction from their priests and paid fees only for such sacrifices as were offered. In the Corinthian correspondence Paul stresses the fact that though he himself had not insisted on remuneration for his services, it is a right which belongs to the Christian teacher. The expectation of financial support in the preaching of the Gospel is, he contends, as natural as the expectation of a farmer to reap the harvest of his work: "He that ploweth ought to plow in hope, and he that thresheth, to thresh in hope of partaking. If we sowed unto you spiritual things, is it a great matter if we shall reap your carnal things?" (1 Cor. 9:10, 11).

Verses 7 and 8, which contain both a warning and a promise, seem to relate primarily to the matter of support or non-support of the Christian ministry. That is to say, Paul appears here to be enforcing the appeal of the preceding verse. If so, he is teaching that a selfish and unsympathetic attitude toward ministers of the Gospel must necessarily result in a harvest of spiritual leanness and that a generous and compassionate attitude toward them will be richly rewarded. But although this is the primary message of these two verses the principle contained in them has a broader application to all that Paul has discussed in this chapter. Viewed in this manner, the passage states a general principle pointing up the consequences of failure to assume one's responsibilities toward his brethren, be they Christian teachers or others. It is an inexorable law of nature that the harvest is directly related to the seed sown. *Be not deceived; God is not mocked: for whatsoever a man soweth, that shall he also reap* (verse 7). The opening words alert the readers to the seriousness of the matter under discussion. They need to know what is at stake. The verb in the expression "God is not mocked" literally suggests turning up one's nose. Paul's statement implies that one who attempts to avoid the consequences of his own moral action is showing contempt for God. God is not to be sneered at. He sees to it that a man reaps what he sows.

One cannot escape reaping the harvest appropriate to his deeds: *He that soweth unto his own flesh shall of the flesh reap corruption; but he that soweth unto the Spirit shall of the Spirit reap eternal life* (verse 8, ASV). "Flesh" in this verse stands for the lower nature (cf. 5:13, 16, 17, 19, etc.). To "sow" to the flesh is to make the flesh (the lower, sinful nature) the seed plot which one cultivates. To put it another way, one who sows to the flesh permits his lower nature to govern his conduct. Such a course of action can result only in a harvest of "corruption," that is, moral and spiritual ruin.

To sow "unto the Spirit" is to yield oneself to the influence of the

Holy Spirit and to let Him govern conduct. Such a course of action results in a harvest of "eternal life." This expression, set in contrast to "corruption," here emphasizes the everlastingness of the life reaped by the Christian. We should not, however, think of eternal life as *only* endless existence. In Scripture, particularly in the writings of John, the term denotes life of a new and different quality. It is a life that is full and rich, a life spiritual and God-like, a life begun here and perfected hereafter.

IV. DOING GOOD TO ALL (6:9, 10).

And let us not be weary in well-doing: for in due season we shall reap, if we faint not (verse 9, ASV). The primary reference is probably to the matter previously discussed, that is, the financial support of those in Christian ministry. The statement is, however, broader than that. It promises a harvest of good to those who persist in well-doing, whatever the well-doing may be. Since this is so, Paul concludes by saying: *So then, as we have opportunity* [the Greek word is the same as that rendered "season," vs. 9], *let us work that which is good toward all men, and especially toward them that are of the household of the faith* (verse 10, ASV). Verse 9 affirms that there is a "due season" for spiritual reaping; this verse suggests that there is also a season (time, opportunity) for sowing, and we must utilize it properly. Paul assumes that such opportunities will come. When they do, we are to work that which is good toward *all* men but are to be especially mindful of those who belong to the Christian fellowship.

The reference to "the household of faith" suggests that all believers belong to one spiritual family. We are to cultivate this family relationship by doing good to one another.

With these words, the main body of the epistle is brought to a close. What remains is in the form of a postscript.

FOR FURTHER STUDY

1. List ways in which Christians may bear one another's burdens.
2. List ways in which we may do good to all men.
3. Read Maclaren's sermon on "Burden-Bearing" in his *Expositions of Holy Scripture*. George W. Truett has a great sermon on the same text entitled "What to Do with Life's Burdens." See his *A Quest for Souls*.

CHAPTER 11

The Epilogue

(Galatians 6:11-18)

Paul customarily dictated his letters to an amanuensis (cf. Rom. 16:22) and then, taking the pen in hand, attached his signature as an authentication of the whole letter (cf. Col. 4:18; 2 Thess. 3:17). It would appear that in this letter, however, he was not content simply to add the signature. Instead, he puts down a sort of postscript to which he attaches great importance. In it there are three things: (1) a resume of the main message of the Galatian letter (verses 11-16), (2) a personal appeal (verse 17), and (3) a benediction (verse 18).

I. A RESUME OF THE LETTER (6:11-16).

In his resume of the letter Paul repeats his warning against the Judaizers (verses 12, 13), reiterates the doctrine of the cross and his confidence in it (verses 14, 15), and closes with a prayer of peace and mercy for all those who make up the Israel of God (verse 16).

Taking the pen in order to write his concluding remarks in his own hand, Paul first draws attention to the large letters with which he is writing: *See with how large letters I write unto you with mine own hand* (verse 11, ASV). (Observe the difference between this translation and that of KJV, which has "how large *a letter I have written*." The use of "large letters" indicates the importance which Paul attached to the things about to be written.

1. *The warning against the Judaizers* (verses 12, 13). Paul affirms that those who were troubling the Galatians were inspired by selfish motives: *As many as desire to make a fair show in the flesh, they compel you to be circumcised; only that they may not be persecuted for the cross of Christ* (verse 12, ASV). Their main concern is to turn aside the hostility of the Jews and to avoid persecution for the cross of Christ.

"To make a fair show in the flesh" means that the Judaizers want to put on a good face, "to cut a good figure" (Ridderbos, p. 222), so as to be popular. The TCNT: "Those who wish to appear to advantage in regard to outward observances. . . ."

In verse 13 Paul accuses his opponents of insincerity. *For not even they who receive circumcision do themselves keep the law; but they desire to have you circumcised, that they may glory in your flesh* (ASV). "They who receive circumcision" are the Judaizing teachers. They pretend to be zealous for the law, but even they fail to carry out all of its burdensome restrictions. In making this statement, Paul seems not to be thinking of the general inability of men to keep the law, but of the hypocrisy which characterized the Judaizers. Ostensibly they are zealous for the law, but their real concern is for themselves. They want to boast in the fact that they have made Gentiles knuckle under to Judaism.

2. *The centrality of the cross* (verses 14, 15).[1] *Far be it from me to glory, save in the cross of our Lord Jesus Christ* (verse 14a, ASV). This is Paul's way of saying that whereas the Judaizers are ashamed of the cross, underrate its importance, and seek in every possible way to avoid persecution for the sake of it, he himself glories in it. The verb suggests the ideas of pride and joy, but perhaps the main thought in this context is that Paul makes the cross the grounds of his confidence. Through it, he says, *the world hath been crucified unto me, and I unto the world* (verse 14b, ASV). Paul means by this that it was the propitiatory death of Christ upon the cross, and his participation in that death, that had made him dead to the world and the world dead to him. Burton thinks the "world" of which Paul speaks is that of Jewish rites, the world of legalism. Paul has through the cross died to that world, and it has to him become as a dead thing, that is, has lost all claim on him. Perhaps it is better to understand the "world" here in a broader sense, that is, as the "epitome of everything outside of Christ in which man seeks his glory and puts his trust" (Ridderbos, p. 224). Because of the cross this whole world has died to Paul. It has lost all significance, all attraction for him.

This leads Paul to the statement of another sweeping principle: *For neither is circumcision anything, nor uncircumcision, but a new*

---

[1] The vocabulary of verses 14 and 15 is strikingly Pauline. The Greek for "Far be it from me" (KJV, "God forbid") is used fifteen times in the New Testament, but all but one of these occurrences are in Paul. "Crucify," outside of the Gospels, is used only by Paul, except for two short instances in Acts and one in Revelation. "Cross," outside of the Gospels, is used only by Paul except for one reference in Hebrews. The word for "glory" is employed thirty-five times in Paul, twice in James, and nowhere else in the New Testament.

creature (verse 15, ASV). The cross makes both circumcision and un-circumcision religiously meaningless. Circumcision, Paul had come to believe, was nothing more than an external mark in a man's body, and there could be no religious significance in that. All that really matters is that people be made new creatures (lit., "a new creation") in Christ Jesus. This can come about only through faith in Christ.

Paul closes this paragraph with a fervent wish that peace and mercy shall be upon *as many as shall walk by this rule* (verse 16a, ASV). By "rule" we are to understand the principle enunciated in the preceding verse. Those who "walk" (i.e., live) by this rule are those who put all their hope for acceptance with God in the redeeming work of Christ.

The words *and upon the Israel of God* (verse 16b, ASV) are not to be interpreted as referring to a class of Christians different from those described as walking by the rule of faith. It is, like the other ex-pression, a way of describing all who depend on Christ for salvation. They are the spiritual Israel and the true heirs of the promises made to Abraham.

II. A PERSONAL APPEAL (6:17).

Paul feels that he can say nothing more and can do nothing more to check the influence of the Judaizers. He will leave the matter with his readers. He does, however, have one further request to make: *Henceforth let no man trouble me; for I bear branded on my body the marks of Jesus* (verse 17, ASV). The abruptness of the words in-dicates something of the depth of the apostle's feeling. He wishes to be spared further distress and calls attention to the scars which he bears in his body as indications of his devotion to Jesus.

The word for "marks," used only here in the New Testament, sometimes denoted a tattoo or a brand mark. Among the ancients three classes of persons wore such marks: soldiers, slaves, and devotees to the service of pagan temples. Paul's marks, that is, the scars which had been left in his flesh by scourgings, stonings, and hardships endured for the sake of Christ, were evidences that he belonged to Christ. He sees himself as Christ's soldier, Christ's slave, Christ's devotee.

In using this term Paul may be alluding to the fact that the Judaizers made circumcision a mark of their religious status. The apostle affirms that the scars left on his body by persecutions are the only outward marks that he needs to verify his relationship to Jesus Christ.

III. THE BENEDICTION (6:18).

Paul closes his letter with a prayer: *The grace of our Lord Jesus Christ be with your spirit, brethren. Amen* (verse 18, ASV). "Grace," of course, is the favor of God, the kindness which He shows to sinners in and through Jesus Christ. The use of the word "brethren" adds a final touch of affection. Paul has had some severe things to say in his letter, but he wants the readers to know that he does not regard them as enemies, but as brothers.

Of the letters of Paul only Galatians and Romans are closed with the "Amen." It seems to be used in both places to add a note of solemn earnestness: "So be it."

FOR FURTHER STUDY

1. Using Galatians 6:11-15 as a basis, summarize briefly the message of Galatians.

2. Explain why Paul gloried in the cross.

3. Read Spurgeon's sermon on "Three Crosses" (Gal. 6:14) in *The Treasury of the New Testament.*

4. See Maclaren's sermon on Galatians 6:17, "The Owner's Brand."

Bibliography

Adeney, W. F., *Thessalonians and Galatians* in "The Century Bible" (London: Blackwood, Le Bas & Co., n.d.).

Barclay, William, *Galatians and Ephesians* in the "Daily Study Bible" (Philadelphia: The Westminster Press, 1958).

Burton, E. de Witt, *A Critical and Exegetical Commentary on the Epistle to the Galatians* in "The International Critical Commentary" (Edinburgh: T. & T. Clark, 1921).

Cole, R. A., *The Epistle of Paul to the Galatians* in "The Tyndale New Testament Commentaries" (Grand Rapids: William B. Eerdmans Publishing Company, 1965).

Duncan, G. S., *The Epistle of Paul to the Galatians* in "The Moffatt New Testament Commentaries" (New York: Harper and Row, Publishers, n.d.).

Eerdman, Charles, *The Epistle of Paul to the Galatians* (Philadelphia: The Westminster Press, 1930).

Findlay, George G., *Galatians* in "The Expositor's Bible" (New York: Hodder and Stoughton, n.d.).

Guthrie, Donald, *Galatians* in "The Century Bible: New Series" (London: Thomas Nelson & Sons, 1969).

Hovey, Alvah, *Galatians* in "The American Commentary" (Philadelphia: The American Baptist Publication Society, n.d.).

Hunter, A. M., *The Layman's Bible Commentary* (Richmond: John Knox Press, 1959).

Lightfoot, J. B., *St. Paul's Epistle to the Galatians*. Reprint edition (Grand Rapids: Zondervan Publishing House, n.d.).

Mackenzie, W. Douglas, *Galatians and Romans* in "The Westminster New Testament" (New York: Fleming H. Revell Co., 1912).

Ramsay, Sir William M., *A Historical Commentary on St. Paul's Epistle to the Galatians* (New York: G. P. Putnam's Sons, 1900).

Rendall, Frederic, *The Epistle to the Galatians* in "The Expositor's Greek Testament" (Grand Rapids: Wm. B. Eerdmans Publishing Company, n.d.).

Ridderbos, H. N., *The Epistle of Paul to the Churches of Galatia* in "The New International Commentary on the New Testament" (Grand Rapids: Wm. B. Eerdmans Publishing Company, 1954).

Sanday, William, *Galatians* in "Ellicott's Commentary on the Whole Bible." Reprint edition (Grand Rapids: Zondervan Publishing House, n.d.).

Stott, John R. W., *The Message of Galatians* (London: Inter-Varsity Press, 1968).

Williams, A. L., *The Epistle to the Galatians* in "The Cambridge Greek Testament" (Cambridge: The University Press, 1910).

All Scriptures, unless otherwise identified, are quoted from the King James Version. Other translations referred to are as follows:

Bruce, F. F., *The Letters of Paul: An Expanded Paraphrase* (Grand Rapids: Wm. B. Eerdmans Publishing Company, 1965).

Conybeare, W. J., *The Epistles of Paul* (Grand Rapids: Baker Book House, n.d.).

Goodspeed, Edgar J., *The New Testament: An American Translation* (Chicago: The University of Chicago Press, 1951).

Moffatt, James, *The New Testament: A New Translation* (New York: Harper & Brothers, 1950).

Norlie, Olaf M., *The New Testament: A New Translation* (Grand Rapids: Zondervan Publishing House, 1961).

Phillips, J. B., *The New Testament in Modern English* (New York: The Macmillan Company, 1962).

Weymouth, Richard Francis, *The New Testament in Modern Speech.* Newly Revised by James Alexander Robertson (New York: Harper & Brothers, Publishers, n.d.).

Williams, Charles B., *The New Testament: A Private Translation in the Language of the People* (Chicago: Moody Press, 1949).

The New English Bible: New Testament (Oxford & Cambridge: University Press, 1964). Referred to in the Study Guide as NEB.

Good News for Modern Man: The New Testament in Today's English Version (New York: American Bible Society, n.d.). Referred to in the Study Guide as TEV.

The Holy Bible: Revised Standard Version (Grand Rapids: Zondervan Publishing House, 1952). Referred to in the Study Guide as RSV.

The Holy Bible: Standard Edition (New York: Thomas Nelson & Sons, 1929). Referred to in the Study Guide as ASV.

The Twentieth Century New Testament: A Translation into Modern English (Chicago: Moody Press, n.d.). Referred to in the Study Guide as TCNT.

ORDER

BIBLE STUDY COMMENTARIES
The Ideal Commentary for Study Groups

Old Testament

☐ Genesis (Wood) — 34743-2
☐ Exodus (Huey) — 36053-6
☐ Leviticus (Goldberg) — 41813-5
☐ Joshua (Enns) — 44041-6
☐ Job (Garland) — 24863-9
☐ Isaiah (Garland) — 24853-1
☐ Jeremiah (Huey) — 36063-3
☐ Daniel (Wood) — 34723-8
☐ Amos (Garland) — 24833-7
☐ Hosea (Garland) — 24843-4
☐ Malachi (Isbell) — 41673-6

New Testament

☐ Matthew (Vos) — 33883-2
☐ Mark (Vos) — 33873-5
☐ Luke (Gideon) — 24973-2
☐ John (Hobbs) — 26113-9
☐ Acts (Vaughan) — 33513-2
☐ Romans (Vaughan/Corley) — 33573-6
☐ Galatians (Vaughan) — 33543-4
☐ Ephesians (Vaughan) — 33533-7
☐ Philippians (Vos) — 33863-8
☐ Colossians and Philemon (Vaughan) — 33523-X
☐ Thessalonians (Walvoord) — 34071-3
☐ Pastoral Epistles, The (Blaiklock) — 21233-2
☐ James (Vaughan) — 33553-1
☐ I, II, III John (Vaughan) — 33563-9

Visit your local bookstores or call toll free

1-800-253-4475

RETAIL MARKETING SERVICES
1420 Robinson Rd., S.E.
Grand Rapids, MI 49506